Border Line

BORDER LIFE

Travels between
Mexico and the USA

Simon Courtauld

LIBRI MUNDI
LONDON

Elliott & Thompson
London & Bath

for Philippa

Acknowledgments

Many people gave me valuable assistance during my travels and research for this book; a few of them are named in the text. I would like especially to thank Andres Rozental, who shared with me his knowledge of border affairs, as former Mexican government minister and presidential envoy; Dick Roberts and his son Barry, who pointed me in several useful directions in south Texas, and Dick's wife, Bobby, who gave me access to her Mexican library. I am also grateful for their help, whether along the border, in Mexico City or in England, to: Roxy and Jerry Barnett, John Blymeyer, Gioconda Cicogna, Gene Cockrill, Marie-Pierre Colle, Christopher Gill, Lourdes Heredia, Barry Horn, James McAllen, Alexander Maitland, Renee Marcus, Nicholas Mavroleon, Luz Maria Montaño, Miguel Monterrubio, Antonio Obregón, Lady Polwarth, Otto Schwarz and Jerry Thompson.

For permission to use the sculpture *Vaquero* by Luis Jiménez which is reproduced on the cover, I am grateful to the artist, the El Paso Museum of Art and Frank Ribelin.

Contents

	Preface	6
	Map	8
Chapter I	Remember the Alamo!	11
Chapter II	Goings-on at the Gulf	35
Chapter III	Mexican Texas	57
Chapter IV	Slow Train to Misery Pass	89
Chapter V	Pancho Villa Rides Again	109
Chapter VI	Desert and the Devil's Road	125
Chapter VII	California Dreaming	157
Chapter VIII	Mexican Habits Die Hard	177
Chapter IX	A Brighter Border Future?	197
	Envoi	213
	Bibliography	219
	Index	220

Preface

Until 1999, I had never been to the Mexican–American border. Indeed I hadn't been to Mexico, or to any of the American states – Texas, New Mexico, Arizona, California – which adjoin Mexico's northern boundary. I dimly remembered a line from a song – 'South of the border, down Mexico way' – but knew little of that country except that it was liable to get itself massively into debt. I wasn't quite as ignorant as Gavin Young who, on his first visit to Texas, thought the Alamo was a river; but I was not much better informed about Mexican–American history. It was the Alamo massacre, I soon learned, that led to the rolling back of the frontiers of Old Mexico (or New Spain, as it had been until the early nineteenth century) from the Gulf of Mexico to the Pacific Ocean. I resolved to travel along that border, which had remained unchallenged for the last hundred and fifty years, from Brownsville/Matamoros next to the Gulf to the Pacific cities of San Diego/Tijuana two thousand miles away. It was my intention to observe the life of two peoples, one living in the Third World, the other in the First, who share the same Hispanic heritage; to learn a bit more history; and to find out about the two principal border issues of today – illegal immigration and the drugs traffic.

It was, for the most part, a leisurely journey, undertaken in stages, by car, bus and train. I did not travel every mile of the border; more intrepid travellers might have taken to a boat on the Rio Grande to negotiate the canyons of the Big Bend, or tried to infiltrate one of the Mexican drug cartels. But I believe I have come to some understanding of this unique borderland. It was for me partly a journey of discovery, and as it progressed and both countries elected new presidents, I looked upon it, too, as a journey of hope for Mexico's illegal immigrants. Both Vicente Fox and George Bush were talking in terms of a new deal for immigrants and a new bi-national approach to border problems. Then came the Arab terrorist attacks on New York and Washington. For the foreseeable future, Muslim immigrants, as suspected followers of Osama bin Laden, were going to take priority on President Bush's agenda; the interests of Mexican immigrants no longer appeared important. Nor, in the context of America's war against this hidden enemy, was Congress likely to support a programme to legalise the status of several million immigrants in the USA. However, as Bush reminded Fox less than a week before September 11th, in 1861 Abraham Lincoln had paused in the darkest hour of his country's history to send a word of encouragement to Mexico which had just been invaded by forces from France. In the first months of 2001, Presidents Bush and Fox evinced a vast change in attitude towards each other's countries and towards a shared solution to border issues. So it was reasonable for Mexicans to hope that George W. Bush would find time, in another of the nation's darkest hours, to send them a reassuring message. I remain optimistic that the immigrants' lot will be improved, though it may now take longer than anticipated. But Mexicans are used to waiting.

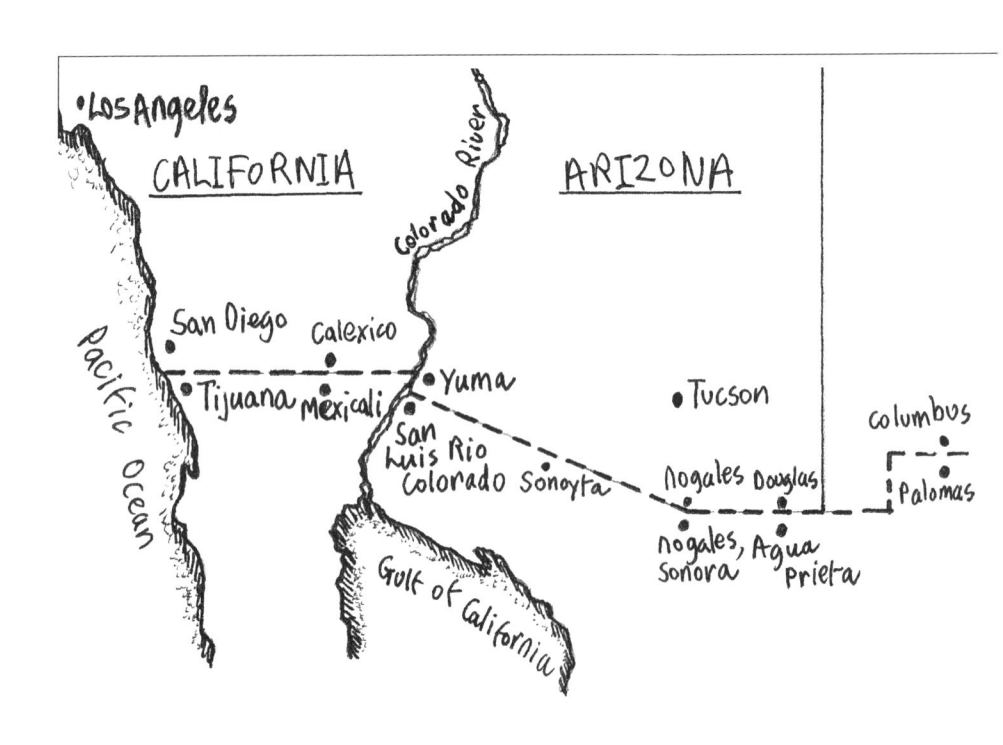

The United States Border with Mexico

NEW MEXICO
Dallas
Pecos River
TEXAS
El Paso
Ciudad Juarez
Rio Grande
Rio Bravo
San Antonio
Presidio
Ojinaga
Rio Conchos
Del Rio
Ciudad Acuña
Eagle Pass
Corpus Christi
Piedras Negras
Laredo
Nuevo Laredo
Gulf of Mexico
MEXICO
Rio Grande City
McAllen
Brownsville
Camargo
Reynosa
Matamoros

Alamo chapel, San Antonio

Chapter One

Remember the Alamo!

In memory of the heroes who sacrificed their lives at the Alamo, March 6 1836, in the defense of Texas. They chose never to surrender nor retreat; these brave hearts, with flag still proudly waving, perished in the flames of immortality that their high sacrifice might lead to the founding of this Texas.

From the fire that burned their bodies rose the eternal spirit of sublime heroic sacrifice which gave birth to an empire state.

As THE largest state of the Union (excluding Alaska) and one with a penchant for superlatives, Texas could be expected to go a bit over the top in its inscriptions on the Alamo memorial in San Antonio, constructed for the centenary of the battle. The monument itself, standing a few yards from part of the low wall which surrounded the mission chapel of the Alamo fortress, is typically huge and overpowering. And, with its outsize marble figures which include one ascending Phoenix-like from the burning pyre, it lacks a certain dignity and restraint. The names of the 183 who died at the Alamo are inscribed on the base: they include those of William Travis, the quixotic commander of the Texan garrison, James Bowie, a drunken knife fighter, David (Davy) Crockett, 'the Coonskin Congressman', several English, Scots and Irish and a number of Mexicans – Antonio Fuentes, Juan Abamillo, Andres Nava – who fought against their countrymen.

⇢ Remember the Alamo! ⇠

The same names are all listed, too, in the sympathetically restored, and much more impressive, eighteenth-century Alamo chapel – making the 1936 memorial outside rather redundant. Here is a true feeling of history (even if the hunting musket said to have belonged to Crockett and displayed in a glass case is probably not the 'Old Betsy' which he always used). One of the Heroes of the Alamo on a wall plaque is named only as 'John —, negro'. Whether or not they realised it at the time, the 183 were making a high and heroic sacrifice not only for the future of the 'empire state' of Texas, but for nine other states or parts of states which, twelve years later, were to be taken from Mexico and incorporated into the Union. It was one of the greatest land grabs in history, outside the British Empire, adding almost a million square miles to the area of the United States and leaving a Mexican, and Spanish, legacy which endures today. Since 1848, Mexico has been gradually reconquering the gringos, as Carlos Fuentes has written, 'with the most Mexican of weapons, linguistic, racial and culinary'.

When Graham Greene was in San Antonio in the 1930s, he thought it more Mexican than American; and he was struck by the conditions of poverty endured by Mexicans there who spent all day shelling pecan nuts for a few cents. Today the vast majority of San Antonio's residents are of Mexican blood (Chicanos); *enchiladas* and *fajitas* are more popular, among both Chicanos and 'Anglos', than steak and shrimp; and the Spanish language is commonly spoken. Negroes and Muslims are rarely seen (so that it was a surprise to learn that three Arabs were attending a San Antonio flying school before the terrorist attacks of 11 September 2001. One might have thought that, in Hispanic Texas, they would at least have attracted some attention.)

At the Menger Hotel in Alamo Plaza, where Colonel Theodore Roosevelt recruited some of his 'Rough Riders' to go to Cuba and fight the Spanish in 1898, entrances and exits are also marked *entrada* and *salida*. The main covered market in San Antonio deals almost entirely in Mexican goods – ponchos, sombreros, ceramics, lots of leather, papier maché objects, raccoon- and coyote-skin bags. One stall was selling knives which looked fearsome enough for any Mexican *bandido*. On the same counter were metal alloy 'stress balls' – whether intended for the knife-fighters or their likely victims it was hard to say. In public life Mexican Texans are increasingly being appointed to positions of authority, prompting some of them to claim that Mexico is making a comeback – while others say privately that the United States should have taken a lot more of that miserable country. On the car radio one day, from one of a number of Spanish-speaking channels, I heard the Battle Hymn of the Republic sung in Spanish. If some of this tends to be confusing, a little history may help.

A few of the first conquering Spaniards were exploring in these parts (what is now south Texas) as early as the 1530s. One Alvar Núñez, better known as Cabeza de Vaca (Cow's Head), came ashore near the Mississippi delta and spent several years wandering westward, and enduring great hardship, before he finally reached Mexico City. When he crossed the Rio Grande he reported that it reminded him of the Rio Guadalquivir in his home town of Seville. In those days the lower Rio Grande may have been about two hundred yards wide; today it is seldom more than fifty. Franciscan fathers – they were the most important missionary order in New Spain – moved into the area in the early eighteenth century, establishing Catholic missions as they went. One, which was founded in 1718 and called San Antonio de Valero (after St Anthony of Padua and the Marquess of Valero, viceroy of Mexico), became better known as Alamo, meaning cottonwood tree, a species of American poplar. Until after the Alamo siege, the city of San Antonio, by then the capital of Texas, was called after Valero's brother, the Duke of Bejar (Bexar), who took his name from a town in the foothills of the Sierra de Gredos west of Madrid.

The first settlement on the San Antonio River was established in

1731, when fifteen families arrived from the Canary Islands. By 1747 the region of Nuevo Santander, extending east and west of the Rio Grande, had come into being; its first town was Camargo, on the right bank of the river. Other settlements were founded and given names of towns – Laredo, Reinosa – close to Santander in Spain. With grants of land from King Charles III, more Spanish families came from the Cantabrian north. They were encouraged to settle west of the Mississippi to deter the French from moving into Spanish territory from Louisiana, which they had recently ceded to Spain; and the Catholic missions served as fortresses against threatened incursions from the east by the English as well as the French. By 1821 permission had been granted by the Spanish viceroy in Mexico for Anglo-American families to settle in Texas, provided they were Catholic and obeyed Spanish law. Later that same year, however, Mexico won its independence from Spain and for the next fifteen years Texas came under Mexican rule.

The seeds of the Mexican revolt had been sown more than fifty years earlier, when all Jesuits were expelled from Mexico. They had done much to civilise and educate the natives, and their deportation was especially resented by the *criollos* (those of Spanish blood who were born in Mexico). As the antagonism worsened between *criollos* and *peninsulares* (those born in Spain), the former suffered from commercial restrictions imposed on them by the Spanish immigrants, who ran an administrative system which, in view of what has gone on in Mexico ever since, can best be described as irredeemably corrupt. It was in some respects a class struggle, and the underclass was helped in its cause by a string of incompetent viceroys in the closing years of the century and by the unrest in Spain occasioned by Joseph Bonaparte's usurping the throne. The first armed rebellion was led by a priest, Miguel Hidalgo, in 1810, then taken up by another holy father, José María Morelos, who suffered defeat in a terrible siege which took place on 2 May 1812 – four years to the day after the great revolutionary rising by the mob in Madrid. But Morelos's forces overran southern Mexico the following year; he called a congress which declared independence, but he was captured and executed in 1815. Spanish rule was re-established, but the advent of a liberal government in Spain caused some Spaniards to fear for their future, and in 1821 they persuaded a conservative general, Agustín de Itúrbide, who had helped suppress the recent guerrilla warfare, to lead what was initially a somewhat reactionary revolution. Itúrbide decided on a constitutional monarchy for this newly independent country and had himself crowned emperor, generously – but unwisely – declaring national holidays on the birthdays of each of his eight children. It was no great surprise that he was forced to abdicate after less than a year and was deported to Italy, but he was foolish enough to turn round and come back to Mexico, where he was at once arrested and executed. Mexico now became a federal republic and for the next fifty years was involved in almost continuous warfare. The prediction of the explorer and scientist Baron von Humboldt, who gave his name to the cold current which runs up the Pacific coast, that Mexico would become a greater power than the United States, never really had a chance of being fulfilled.

In Texas there was no immediate problem. The Mexican republic confirmed the territorial concession granted by Spain, and immigration continued. (Crossing the Sabinas River, the new Texans became the first 'wetbacks', years before Mexicans began crossing the Rio Grande to settle in the USA – a point which it would be inadvisable to make in Texas today.) But within a few years most of the incoming English-speaking whites did not meet the requirement that they be Catholic; and to make matters worse they brought their negro slaves with them (slavery was outlawed in Mexico). Mexico had been oddly indulgent towards these settlers invading its territory – by 1830, seventy-five per cent of the population of Texas was American – so that it was hardly surprising when in that year the government banned any further immigration, having already joined Texas to Coahuila, south of the Rio Grande, to form a single state of the Mexican federation. America had offered to buy Texas from Mexico, and there were increasing calls for Texan independence. In 1833, Stephen Austin, whose father had obtained the first grant of land for an American colony in Texas, went to Mexico City to negotiate for a separate Texan state. But a letter in which he recommended proclaiming independence without waiting for the Mexican government to agree was intercepted. When Austin was arrested on the way home and held prisoner for a year, it became inevitable that armed hostilities would soon follow.

San Antonio in 1835 was occupied by Mexican soldiers under the command of General Perfecto de Cos. Stories at the time relate that when a Colonel Benjamin Milam heard that the garrison's morale was low and food was short, he uttered the rallying cry, 'Who will come with Old Ben Milam into San Antonio?' and was at once joined by 250 American troops. After four days of street fighting, Cos withdrew, but by this time Old Ben was dead, shot by a sniper from a cypress tree. Two months later, a Mexican force of some 4,500, led by the country's dictator president (and Cos's brother-in-law), General Antonio López de Santa Anna, crossed the Rio Grande and headed for San Antonio to teach those seceding Texans a lesson. The entire garrison of the old Catholic mission, which was now a half-ruined fortress known as the Alamo, was slaughtered.

There is so much folklore and myth surrounding the Alamo battle that it is almost impossible to be sure of some of the details. It may be easier to stay with the personalities. According to Walter Lord's very readable account, *A Time to Stand*, the previous commander of the Alamo garrison, Colonel Neil, had been ordered some weeks before the battle by the Texas commander-in-chief, Sam Houston, to abandon the old mission and blow it up. It was James Bowie, the bearer of these instructions from Houston to Neil, who decided not to allow the fort to be destroyed; he began rebuilding its walls and reviving the morale of its defenders. Bowie was a maverick frontiersman – the word 'maverick' derives from a Texas rancher, Sam Maverick, who let his cattle roam at will without being branded – who had moved west from New Orleans, bringing his collection of hunting knives and getting drunk along the way. His was the moving spirit behind the resolve to try and hold the Alamo against a vastly superior force; but he did not take command. When Neil decided to quit he was replaced by Colonel William Travis, who arrived with reinforcements. Bowie did not get on with Travis but had to submit to his authority after being laid low with pneumonia – from which he was still suffering at the end.

In the 1960 film *The Alamo*, produced and directed by John Wayne, who also played Crockett, Richard Widmark played Bowie as an attractive, gregarious figure, married to a wealthy Creole Spaniard. In complete contrast was Travis, whom Laurence Harvey portrayed as a loner, autocratic and awkward, a heroic failure somewhat in Scott-of-the-Antarctic mould, and with some of Captain Scott's characteristics. Travis and Bowie are constantly at odds with one another in the film, apparently reflecting their actual relationship. Crockett, on the other hand, though no less of a maverick than Bowie, is respected and liked by Travis. As director of the film, Wayne ensures that Crockett is one of the last to die, while igniting the rest of the garrison's powder barrels. It is not known how Crockett in fact met his end: it has been whispered by historians that he surrendered before he was shot, but this is not something to be raised in Texan company. Everyone is agreed, however, on one point: all 183 male defenders of the Alamo fort were killed. The final assault was preceded by Mexican bugles calling the *deguello* (literally, throat-cutting), which signified that no Americans would be spared.

If much of America was horrified by the wholesale slaughter, it was the death of Crockett which moved people most. The *Natchez Courier* commented:

> Poor Davy Crockett… It is too bad – by all that is good, it is too bad. The quaint, the laughter-moving, the fearless upright Crockett, to be butchered by such a wretch as Santa Anna - it is not to be borne.

He was already something of a national hero – a sharp-shooting backwoodsman from Tennessee who went on to serve his state as a congressman in Washington. He had an endearing, swashbuckling style, and he wore buckskin shoes and shirt and a coonskin cap. At the congressional elections in 1835 he was said to have told his constituents that if they didn't re-elect him, 'You can go to hell – I shall go to Texas.' Which he did, arriving in San Antonio with a band of hell-raising followers to the welcoming roar of a cannon and the playing of 'Hail the Conquering Hero'. There was no more conquering to be done, but he died a hero – of course – in his fiftieth year, and has had streets, a town, a county and a national forest named after him.

Heroic these freedom-fighting frontiersmen may have been in sacrificing their lives for Texas, but few could call themselves Texans, and for the most part they were not soldiers but an ill-disciplined rabble. Which may make their sacrifice all the more romantic; but one may sympathise with the irritation felt by some Mexican Americans today. The Alamo battle was not so much a case of black (Mexico) against white (Texas), as of a legitimate government against a motley band of Americans from distant parts of the Union, who should have been Mexican citizens subject to Mexican law and customs. Independent Mexico was, after all, seeking to retain control over a part of its territory which was threatened by the invasion of rebellious foreigners, most of whom practised slavery and paid no taxes to the government. What the recently arrived Texans really objected to was that they were losing their quasi-autonomous status, or what they would call their freedom. The 1824 constitution giving state rights to Texas had been repealed by Santa Anna, who preferred everything to be ordered from Mexico City. In John Wayne's film the Mexican flag flown by the Alamo defenders over their compound is overpainted with the date 1824.

Santa Anna, who came from Veracruz, has been described as neither a general, nor a statesman, nor an honest man. But he was a most remarkable survivor. He was effectively military dictator for about twenty years, with two periods of enforced retirement. In his last two years as head of his troubled country, Santa Anna was made 'president for life' with the title of Most Serene Highness. Exile and the death sentence were no strangers to him but, amazingly, he lived on and died in his bed aged eighty-one. It was the merciless ferocity with which Santa Anna conducted his battles, as much as the restrictions he imposed on Texan freedoms, which made him and his army so hated. Two weeks after the Alamo defeat, another Texan garrison, farther down the San Antonio River at Goliad, was overrun by Mexican forces. The surrender of James Fannin (who had been expected by Travis to relieve his embattled contingent at the Alamo) was followed by the massacre, on Santa Anna's orders, of three hundred and seventy of his four hundred men.

Houston then decided to retreat before Santa Anna, eastwards across the Colorado River and on to the San Jacinto River, where, on 21 April 1836, he routed the Mexicans and brought the war to an end. With a largely untrained force of a few hundred against a Mexican army superior in discipline and numbers, Houston reasoned that his only chance lay in luring Santa Anna into deeply wooded country. But he was greatly assisted when the self-styled Napoleon of the West detached 800 of his men and led them in pursuit of the provisional Texan government, which was said to be fleeing south. When Houston and Santa Anna faced each other, after a forced march in dreadful weather, the

☙ Remember the Alamo! ❧

Americans were no longer outnumbered. Thirsting for revenge, they advanced with cries of 'Remember the Alamo!' and cut down the Mexicans in twenty minutes. Like several of the decisive battles of history, it lasted a very short time: Santa Anna escaped briefly to hide in the marshes, but was taken prisoner the following day. In exchange for his life, he signed a treaty with Houston recognising the independence of Texas and agreeing to withdraw his army for ever beyond the Rio Grande. The independent republic of Texas was proclaimed in September 1836, with Houston as president, and it was annexed to the Union, after lengthy argument over slavery, in 1845. Predictably enough, it did not take Santa Anna long to deny that he had signed Texas away, but he was treated with suspicion when he returned to Mexico. He soon redeemed himself, however, by losing a leg in an attack by the French on his home town of Veracruz, and once again became military dictator in 1841, receiving the title of Benemerito de la Patria. When America invaded in 1846, the wily general, by now an exile living in Cuba, was recalled to command his country's forces. President James Polk was gullible enough to permit Santa Anna's return, lifting the American blockade of the Mexican coast, on his assurance that he would at once settle the boundary dispute peaceably. Unsurprisingly, Santa Anna broke his word, but within two years he had lost once again to the Americans, who this time won many more territorial prizes.

Sam Houston, by then a US senator, took no part in that war. But it is he, not the Heroes of the Alamo, who can be said to have been truly responsible for the founding of Texas, and it is right that Texas's largest city should be named after him. Like Crockett, Houston came from Tennessee, where he spent three years living with Cherokee Indians, whose rights he would later champion in Washington. Houston's political career ended when he refused to swear allegiance to the Confederacy. He may therefore be categorised as something of a liberal;

over the future of Texas his argument was with Santa Anna rather than with the Mexican people.

The argument which led to the Mexican war of 1846-8 principally concerned Texas's western border. The United States claimed the Rio Grande, ceded by Santa Anna ten years earlier, but now the latter insisted that Texas, if it was recognised at all, certainly did not extend beyond the Nueces River, which runs roughly parallel to the Rio Grande, but between fifty and a hundred and fifty miles farther east towards San Antonio. The future twelfth president of the United States, Zachary Taylor, entered the disputed territory, which was settled almost exclusively by Mexicans, and pitched camp near the mouth of the Rio Grande. Here he provocatively proceeded to build a fort (later Brownsville) and blockade the river opposite Matamoros. Taylor had no regard for uniform – he would sometimes wear a Mexican sombrero – but he knew how to fight and to lead. Having defeated the Mexicans in a couple of engagements, he took Matamoros and carried on south to Monterrey.

Taylor's successes continued, most notably when Santa Anna, with four times as many men but inferior artillery, was defeated in mid-winter at Buena Vista, near Saltillo. 'Old Rough and Ready' was the name Taylor was given by his troops, who themselves acquired the name of Gringos from a line in a traditional English folksong, 'Green grow the rushes O', which they adopted as one of their marching songs. Taylor's nomination for the presidency began soon after the battle. American forces, meanwhile, had occupied Upper California and New Mexico, and during 1847 marched from Veracruz to Mexico City. Among those taking part in this campaign were Ulysses S. Grant and Robert E. Lee who, promoted later to generalship, would famously oppose one another in the American Civil War. The taking of the seat of government in September, by greatly outnumbered American troops, was a humiliating defeat for Mexico, which by the treaty of Guadalupe Hidalgo the following year gave up not only Texas, New Mexico and Upper California but also Arizona, Nevada and Utah and parts of Colorado, Wyoming, Kansas and Oklahoma as well. President Polk was prepared to pay $30 million for the acquisition, but Mexico in fact received only half that sum (the United States also took over some $3 million of debt due to its citizens), plus a further $10 million in 1853 (a rather better deal for Mexico, known as the Gadsden Purchase) for another 45,000 square miles of land in what became southern Arizona and New Mexico. Today Mexicans may look back nostalgically on what used to be – they lost, in effect, one half of their country – but there is little lasting resentment. The general feeling is rather one of jealousy at what America has made of its acquisitions and a longing to take advantage of the opportunities it has created. Mexicans may wonder, however, how they came to lose so much to their northern neighbours who, less than a century before, had been inferior both in wealth and development. The answer must surely have something to do with the fact that, since independence, the United States was growing up fast, and democratically (though the trauma of civil war was still to come), while Mexico was not. Its social structure remained rooted in the past: feudal, repressive, latifundist and dominated by the Catholic Church.

As the architect of his country's defeat, Santa Anna once again went into exile (this time in Jamaica) but, following the experience of nineteenth-century Mexican politics, that it is hard to keep a bad man down, he popped up again, as president, in time to negotiate the Gadsden Purchase. However, the $10 million was soon dissipated, and Santa Anna was forced into retirement for the last time in 1855. Only once was he heard of again, when having tried to return to politics he was condemned to death. But he survived to witness the coming to power of another dictator, Porfirio Díaz, who would also die of old age. And something of Santa Anna is preserved to this day in the USA: his wooden leg which, I was told, can be seen in a museum in Indiana.

✦ Remember the Alamo! ✦

After a few more years of war in the 1850s, Benito Juárez, a lawyer of purely Indian blood, who, by Mexican standards, was something of a reforming liberal, emerged as president. In an effort to consolidate the Mexican economy, he decided to suspend all payments for two years on his country's foreign debts – principally to Spain, France and Britain. All three, rather than make a diplomatic protest, sent troops to occupy Veracruz. Britain and Spain soon withdrew; France, however, increased its force by some thirty thousand.

Napoleon III, nephew of the first emperor, had had an idea. Looking for some glorious enterprise beyond Europe, and urged on by his Spanish wife, the Empress Eugénie, he envisaged building an empire in Mexico and even, with the help of the President of Ecuador, establishing a Kingdom of the Andes. The man he had in mind to preside over this venture, who himself dreamt of creating an empire as far south as the River Plate, was the Habsburg Archduke Maximilian (or Archdupe of Napoleon, as he came to be called). Maximilian was the brother of Emperor Franz Joseph, and may have been the illegitimate son of Napoleon Bonaparte's son, the Duke of Reichstadt, who as a child was very briefly, and nominally, Napoleon II. He is thought to have had a liaison with the Empress Sophie of Bavaria in the year before she gave birth to Maximilian; two weeks after the boy was born, Reichstadt died aged twenty-one. Maximilian entered upon a career in the navy, became commander of the Austrian fleet and was largely responsible for creating the naval port of Trieste. But at the age of twenty-seven he retired to a white castle he had had built on a promontory across the bay from Trieste (he had another on an island off Dubrovnik), and there he designed the gardens and wrote poetry. Approaches were made to him to consider the throne of Mexico, but before taking the fateful decision he went off to Brazil on a botanical expedition. When he returned, the lure of Latin America, and the pressure being exerted by his wife Charlotte, daughter of King Leopold I of the Belgians, and by Napoleon III, whose forces had by now taken Mexico City, were too great for Maximilian to resist – in spite of strong advice from his brother, who threatened him with the loss of all his rights in Austria, and from Queen Victoria, who recorded in her diary that she 'did all I could' to stop him going to Mexico.

Maximilian arrived in Mexico City in June 1864 – it was said that rats drove him from his bed on the first night, compelling him to sleep on a billiard table in the palace – and was proclaimed emperor. Juárez took himself and his supporters off to San Luis Potosí, where he set up his capital, and thence farther north to Chihuahua, and to the banks of the Rio Grande at El Paso del Norte (later to be called Ciudad Juárez in his honour), to await developments. Maximilian, with his own Austrian/Belgian army as well as the French garrisons, nominally held sway for a while over two-thirds of the country, but he never really had a chance. His major problem was the United States which, once it had concluded its civil war in the spring of 1865, resolved to enforce the Monroe Doctrine against Maximilian. Washington continued to regard Juárez as the supreme authority in Mexico, and when US troops made threatening movements in the direction of the Rio Grande, Napoleon III decided it was time to pack up and bring his troops home.

Without French backing, Maximilian was urged to abdicate, and one can imagine him longing to be back at his castle of Miramar on the Adriatic. But his wife, now called Empress Carlota, persuaded him to hang on while she went back to Europe to intercede with the French emperor and, when that didn't work, with the Pope. But while she was in Rome she went mad and was of no further use to her husband. In 1867 he moved north of Mexico City to take command of the garrison at Querétaro, a fine colonial city which was and remains better known for the role played by La Corregidora, the governor's wife, in the first struggle for independence in 1810. Here Maximilian was captured and court-martialled, in a theatre, for having taken up arms against the republic. He was shot, with two Mexican generals, on 19 June, at a place called the Hill of Bells, which today is dominated by a huge statue of the man who resumed his position as head of state, Benito Juárez. As he faced a row of raised muskets, Maximilian, determined to die like a good Habsburg, declared, in Spanish: 'I forgive everybody. I pray that everyone may also forgive me and I wish that my blood which is now to be shed may be for the good of the country.' His last words were: 'Viva Mejico! Viva la independencia!'* He had been Emperor of Mexico for three years, almost to the day, and hardly anybody mourned his passing.

After protracted negotiations, his body was brought back to Trieste by the Austrian navy and buried in Vienna in early 1868. Before its return, however, Queen Victoria had heard that the skull, skin and hair had been sold off in lots. 'Too disgusting & disgraceful!!' she wrote. Juárez ruled Mexico for another five troubled years until he died of apoplexy; Napoleon III retired to Chislehurst, in Kent, and died there in 1873; and the insane Empress Carlota lived on in a castle in Belgium for another sixty years. She survived the First World War (so did Napoleon's widow, Empress Eugénie) and died at last in 1927. She and Maximilian had had no children – he had once thought of adopting a grandson of the ephemeral Emperor Itúrbide – but, most intriguingly, Carlota was said to have given birth to a son in Brussels, shortly before Maximilian's death, who became the French General Weygand (first name Maxime) who, with Petain, capitulated to the Germans in 1940. In 2000, she became the subject of an opera, called *Carlota*, by the Texan composer, Robert Avalon. After the Habsburgs' disastrous Mexican enterprise, one might have assumed that no member of the dynasty

• *Four fragments of Manet's painting of the execution can be seen at the National Gallery, London. Manet dressed the firing squad in French uniforms, making the point that France killed Maximilian by abandoning him. The picture was banned from public view during Manet's lifetime.*

would ever set foot in the country again. It was therefore quite a surprise to discover that a great-great-nephew of Maximilian – Felix von Habsburg, born in 1916 – was living in Mexico City at the beginning of the twenty-first century. Six of his seven children were born in Mexico, where he spent much of his life, describing himself as an industrialist and chairman of several Mexican companies.

Following Juárez, Mexico enjoyed a period of relative stability under Porfirio Díaz, who in effect ruled the country as dictator for the next thirty-five years. However, while the economy was stabilised and industries developed through the inflow of foreign capital, the working classes and the Indians were ruthlessly repressed. The Yaqui tribe in particular suffered appalling cruelties. Díaz's policy was to reduce them to starvation and transport them to slavery in Yucatán, at 75 pesos a head. Slightly more (100 pesos) was offered for the ears of a dead Yaqui warrior.

Díaz, who was of mostly Indian origin, came to prominence as a successful military commander during the war against Maximilian and the French. Apart from a four-year period when a stooge was nominally president, he ruled by amending the constitution to permit his continuous re-election. His rigid control of almost every aspect of life in Mexico was such that, like Louis XIV, he was the state. And for those who opposed the Díaz system of government, sudden death would usually follow. This was often at the hands of the *rurales*, the irregular mounted police force established by Díaz to keep the peasants down and silence any dissenting voices in the countryside. Notoriously corrupt and lazy, they would invoke the *ley fuga* to shoot anyone whom they might think was 'trying to escape'. An American, John Kenneth Turner, published a book on the Díaz tyranny, *Barbarous Mexico*, after two years in the country had convinced him that 'it was under Porfirio Díaz that slavery and peonage were re-established in Mexico, and on a more merciless basis than they had rested upon even under the Spanish dons'.

Bribery at every level of society became even more endemic than before: if you did not take the *pan* (bread), it was said, you could expect the *palo* (stick). Unlike many future Mexican presidents, however, Díaz was not considered personally corrupt. For other redeeeming features of this brutal autocrat, it is instructive, or at any rate entertaining, to turn to the works of Mrs Alec Tweedie, an Englishwoman who journeyed through Mexico in the first decade of the twentieth century and met Díaz and his second wife.

> No one ever impressed me more than the President of Mexico. There is a reserved strength, a quiet force about him which commands respect. a kindly gentleness that wins affection. Each time I saw him I learnt some new trait in his character, and felt how immeasurably above ordinary mankind this self-made ruler undoubtedly was.

When she came to give her verdict on Díaz's achievements, Mrs Tweedie put them in her own perspective:

> For the first time in Mexico's history, her inexpressibly troubled history, he brought scrupulous honesty into every corner of public administration. Corruption in every form went down before Díaz. He toiled, and restored, not only national credit, but internal peace. He could, and did, use stern measures. He converted bandits into *rurales*, a splendid body of military police. He created railroad after railroad, harbours, canals, tunnels, drains, an improved system of education – in a word, converted a hopelessly battered into a conspicuously flourishing state.

Accepting that Díaz brought industrial development to Mexico, and improved the country's economy, it was nevertheless the case that by

1907 he was presiding over worsening inflation and declining real wages. Social revolution was not far away. Díaz, now aged eighty, was dithering over the succession, saying he would not stand again for president; but then, in 1910, he had himself re-elected once more, by 'a record margin' (the record being the extent of electoral fraud perpetrated by the government). Meanwhile, rebellion was being raised by an unlikely revolutionary, Francisco Madero, who belonged to one of the richest families in Mexico. When Díaz finally agreed to go, in May 1911, he went quietly but painfully, suffering (Mrs Tweedie tells us) from inflamed abscesses in tooth and ear. But before leaving Mexico City for Veracruz and a German ship which would take him to exile in Europe, he managed to murder another two hundred of his subjects, part of a huge demonstration which turned up outside the National Palace to speed him on his way only to be met by machine-gun fire. The president of thirty-five years lived the last five years of his life in Paris, among the old enemy he had helped defeat fifty years earlier. Mrs Tweedie went to see her hero again, and took him to the Crystal Palace when he came to London. While in Mexico he had hardly ever been inside a church, but he embraced the Catholic faith towards the end.

The Mexican Revolution* was not like others: it did not derive from defeat in war, and it did not result in a great socio-economic upheaval. True, the power of the *Porfiriato*, as the autocratic Díaz set-up was known, and the *hacienda* (the feudal colonial structure of landownership) was broken, and many of the old *hacendados* fled to the USA (for a while). But there was no general agrarian reform, and by 1917 a new constitution was enacted which gave the president rather more powers than Porfirio Díaz had enjoyed (though the president could not go on

---

* *The years of revolution, with particular reference to Pancho Villa and attempts by Germany to involve Mexico in the First World War, are considered further in Chapter Five.*

having himself re-elected). Where Mexico's resembled most other prolonged revolutions was in its capacity for consuming its own. Three of the first four revolutionary presidents were assassinated. One of them (Venustiano Carranza) was complicit in the death of one of the revolution's heroes, Emiliano Zapata; another (Alvaro Obregón) was responsible for the murder of the other heroic figure, Pancho Villa. During the anarchy and civil war which followed the brief reigns of Madero and Victoriano Huerta, Zapata and Villa had their chance to unite the country. They had what would be their only meeting, in Mexico City, which was supposed to lead to an alliance between north and south; but a joint strategy never got off the ground.

Almost the only thing they had in common was their devotion to women or, rather, to womanising. Both of them contracted bogus 'marriages' with a variety of mistresses and sired numerous children. (The youngest of his sons was born shortly after Villa had been shot dead while visiting a mistress.) But there was no meeting of minds between the Centaur of the North and the Attila of the South over revolutionary strategy. Part of the problem was that Villa was always happier in his native Chihuahua, and Zapata never looked beyond his home state of Morelos. From Mexico City the two together could probably have delivered a knockout blow to the likely next president, Carranza, then lurking in Veracruz. But instead Villa headed north, while Zapata returned to his patch.

Unlike the other major participants, Zapata was a true revolutionary, but he had no national vision. (He was given the full Hollywood treatment in a 1952 film, *Viva Zapata!*, starring a luxuriantly moustached Marlon Brando, with screenplay by John Steinbeck and direction by Elia Kazan.) Villa was not a socialist: land reform to him meant taking it from the old *hacendados* and giving it to his followers. 'I would never fight for the equality of the social classes,' he once said. But for nine years he fought and fought and fought again – in pitched battles at

Torreon and Zacatecas (his most memorable victories), in suicidal cavalry charges involving thousands of casualties, in raids all over the mountain and desert state of Chihuahua, and most famously in his invasion of United States territory in March 1916.

The revolution and civil war became largely a power struggle between northerners: Madero, Pascual Orozco, Villa, Carranza, Obregón, Plutarco Elias Calles – all of them were from the states of Sonora, Chihuahua and Coahuila, having borders with the USA. Perhaps there is something in the harsh country and climate of the north, and the history of tension and skirmishing along the international border, which breeds warriors and leaders of men. Felipe Angeles, born in the state of Hidalgo north of Mexico City, was rather different: a cosmopolitan scholar and thinker and a political moderate who had also served as a Villista general. He worked hard for a Villa–Zapata alliance and he might have been the man to lead a government of national reconciliation. Carranza, of course, realised this and arranged for Angeles to go the way of almost all revolutionary leaders in those brutal years. When peace finally broke out, something like a million people, out of a population of fifteen million, had been killed (and another three hundred thousand died in the winter of 1918 from the Spanish flu). Carranza, who had been recognised as president by Woodrow Wilson in 1915, tried to stay on after 1919, but a combination of Obregón and Calles forced him out of Mexico City, and he was murdered in a hill village outside Veracruz.

Obregón, with one arm and a bushy moustache, succeeded to the presidency, with Calles as his minister of the interior. It was the time of the 'finger generals', men who were not career soldiers but had been given high rank during the revolution by means of *dedazo*, pointing the finger, which was to become the standard method of appointing the government candidate for 'election' as the next president. These generals took over large *haciendas*, enriched themselves through a variety of corrupt practices and occasionally threatened military coups. But Obregón enjoyed saying of them: 'There isn't one who can stand up to a cannonade of 25,000 pesos.' When his term came to an end, Calles took over for four years. The idea was for Obregón to return as president in 1928 (for an extended term of six years, which he and Calles had pushed through Congress), but a few weeks after his re-election Obregón was shot dead at a lunch party by a young artist. Both Obregón and Calles undertook some land redistribution, though neither had any intention of making any inroads into capitalist society. What really exercised Calles, dubbed El Jefe Maximo because by 'fingering' his nominal successors he was able to retain power for ten years, was the Catholic Church and its obscurantist refusal to embrace the principles of the revolution.

Anti-clericalism, and the expropriation of church property, went back to Benito Juárez. It was held in abeyance under Porfirio Díaz, but the 1917 constitution restated the anti-clerical policy of the state in uncompromising terms. Article 3 provided for the abolition of church schools and of all religious teaching. Education was to be solely a matter for the state; it was to be socialist, stifling 'fanaticism and prejudices' and encouraging 'an exact and rational conception of the Universe'. The article had not yet been applied, but when the bishops publicly protested against the new constitution and declared their opposition to the unions (Confederacion Regional Obrera Mexicana) which supported the government, Calles decided to act. He began by implementing Article 3 and, in a post-revolutionary move against foreign interference, deported two hundred Spanish priests. Mexican priests were required to register with the civil authorities, but the bishops forbade them to do so and, with approval from Rome, ordered them instead to stop administering the sacraments or saying mass. Outside the major cities, Indians continued to use the churches without benefit of clergy, while in the south-west Catholic guerrilla bands, known as

Cristeros, set fire to the public schools and murdered their lay teachers. The army responded by sacking churches and attacking prominent Catholics. The work of the church was effectively driven underground; those priests who celebrated mass in private houses and garages did so in peril of their lives. One of them, the Jesuit Father Pro, daily gave communion to hundreds of people in Mexico City and successfully avoided the plain-clothes police, once by posing himself as a police officer. When he was caught, he was publicly executed, without trial and in front of photographers. The international outcry was such that the US ambassador persuaded Calles that an accommodation must be reached between church and government. It took time, but after three years priests were able to return to their churches and the Cristero rebellion petered out.

Elsewhere in the country, however, the religious persecution worsened. According to Graham Greene in *The Lawless Roads*, an account of his travels in Mexico during the late 1930s, it was 'the fiercest ... anywhere since the reign of Elizabeth'. In the southern states of Tabasco and Chiapas, churches were pulled down or locked and left to decay. Statues and sacred images were smashed and publicly burned, and priests were hunted down and shot. Churches were still closed when Greene was there in 1938, and the bishops of Tabasco and Chiapas were only allowed to return to their dioceses in that year. Greene's novel *The Power and the Glory* was based on the 'godless state' of Tabasco, where the governor's militia of Red Shirts would habitually kill priests and their congregations before demolishing their church buildings. He tells the story of the last few weeks in the life of an all too human 'whisky priest' hunted to his inevitable execution. This reign of terror continued for a while under Calles's successor, General Lázaro Cárdenas, until he began to adopt different methods, saying he was 'tired of closing churches and finding them full. Now I am going to open the churches and educate the people and in ten years I shall find them empty.' However, he underrated the influence of the Catholic Church, not least among the Indians. When Calles pointed the finger at Cárdenas in 1934, it was on the understanding that he would be no more than a stooge president, prepared to do El Jefe Maximo's bidding. Five years earlier, Calles had brought into being a national political party (Partido Nacional Revolucionario) to perpetuate his policies; but Cárdenas, from a peasant family in Michoacan, belonged to the left wing of the party and did seem genuinely to want to improve the lot of Mexico's underclass. Within eighteen months he had filled his cabinet with his own men and expelled Calles from the country. He admitted twenty-five thousand republicans to Mexico at the end of the Spanish Civil War, and he invited Trotsky to spend his exile in Mexico, where the revolutionary was murdered by a Spanish agent of the Soviet NKVD. The one act which brought Cárdenas universal popularity among his people was the nationalisation of the oil industry in 1938, celebrated each year by a national holiday on 18 March. In view of the British oil companies' stake in Mexico, the Chamberlain government severed diplomatic relations, but only until the war, when Britain needed Mexican oil, whether nationalised or not.

Agreement on compensation, however, was not reached until after 1945, and it was not fully paid for another ten years. Cárdenas kept on popping up in Mexican political life long after his presidential term had come to an end. Sometimes his reappearances were harmless enough, but he did not endear himself to future governments when he began to espouse international Communism, accepting the Stalin Peace Prize and offering to assist Castro in Cuba. (The name of Cárdenas was perpetuated when his son Cuauhtémoc unsuccessfully stood three times for president, between 1988 and 2000. He probably won the 1988 election, but traditional electoral malpractices ensured that the government party candidate, Carlos Salinas, became president.)

❖ Remember the Alamo! ❖

Under Manuel Avila Camacho, Mexico declared war on the Axis in 1942, a few months after the United States, though popular support inclined towards Hitler, if only to annoy the Americans. Roosevelt made the first visit to Mexico of any American president in office. In 1946 Miguel Alemán Valdes began the era of civilian presidents: more corrupt than ever, still fingering one another, but at least the time of the post-revolutionary generals had passed. Foreign investment returned, better regulated this time to Mexican advantage, and female suffrage was introduced in the 1950s; in 1968 student riots broke out, embarrassingly just before the Olympic Games were held in Mexico City. The economy became stronger, thanks to oil, then weaker, due to the decline in world oil prices and massive external debt incurred by borrowing against oil revenues. The peso was devalued, the gap between rich and poor got wider and the country's population doubled, to almost a hundred million, in the last quarter of the century. On the day (1 January 1994) that the North American Free Trade Agreement (NAFTA, with the United States and Canada) came into being, the Zapatista National Liberation Army initiated an armed uprising in Chiapas, one of the poorest southern states, demanding autonomous rights for the country's ten million indigenous people. Mexico's official party, renamed the Partido Revolucionario Institucional (PRI), appeared to be in power in perpetuity; but in the year 2000, Vicente Fox, a former Coca-Cola executive wearing cowboy boots and representing the Partido de Accion Nacional (PAN), succeeded in beating the system and the government candidate. He offered an end to corruption, a new dawn for his country and a new deal for the mass of migrants who continued their exodus to the promised land of the United States. Everyone wanted to believe in him, but he was given only six years in which to change his country's habits of many lifetimes.

Chapter Two

Goings-on at the Gulf

THE RIO GRANDE (so called by Americans) or Rio Bravo del Norte (its full Mexican name) flows into the Gulf of Mexico a few miles beyond Brownsville, Texas and Matamoros, Tamaulipas. This is the end of the river which rises more than two thousand miles away in the mountains of Colorado, but it's the beginning of the frontier between the United States and Mexico. At its mouth, and indeed along the whole of its length, the river today is neither *grande* nor *bravo* (wild). Here it is only about fifty yards wide, with sand-dunes on either side and salt flats stretching into the far distance. The wife of an army officer, coming ashore in the 1850s, described their arrival:

> There was quite a heavy sea on the bar, and the little dinghy brought us near, pitching and tumbling, till at length it seemed to throw us on the sand. I could not perceive a scene more dreary. There is nothing but sand, blown into hillocks here and there, not a blade of grass or the faintest appearance of greenness. A few rough board houses set down at random in the sand, looking as much like very common barns as anything else, completes the picture.

Nothing much has changed over the past century and a half. It is said that Third World meets First World nowhere more abruptly and dramatically than at this international border, but there is no evidence here of any distinction between the two. A few temporary fishing shacks are visible on the Mexican bank, and on both sides there may be fishermen, looking pretty much alike, casting for redfish and flounder. Gulls and terns glide overhead and pelicans skim above the waves offshore. There are no paved roads to bring families for a day on the beach, nor any signs to indicate that this is an international boundary.

It is a peaceful, unspoilt coastal scene – no customs posts, no border fences, no immigrants. The undocumented ones or *indocumentados* ('*mojados*' or 'wetbacks' are now deemed politically incorrect terms, though widely used, not least by the Mexicans themselves) do sometimes make the crossing at the river mouth, but it is not recommended. A local birdwatcher told me he had once seen three people standing on a sandbar whose purpose was evident by the fact that they were carrying not fishing-rods but plastic bags. Once they had forded or been ferried across the river to Texas, they would be unable to get much farther up the coast before meeting the ship channel which goes for seventeen miles inland from the Gulf to the Port of Brownsville. (Most illegal immigrants on this coast, from Central America as well as Mexico, are landed at Port Isabel, just north of the ship channel.) The only alternative is to follow the river back, across salt flats and scrub providing hardly any cover, and head north beyond the port, on the outskirts of Brownsville. The US Border Patrol maintains only three vehicles in this desolate area, which is bisected by the lonely road out to Boca Chica beach. Only an occasional giant yucca or cactus breaks the total flatness of the landscape, which appears to stretch to infinity. But there is history here: volunteers for General Zachary Taylor's army came this way at the start of the Mexican War in 1846, and a remarkable battle was fought on this featureless estuarial plain at the end of the Civil War. It was in fact fought five weeks after General Lee had surrendered at Appomattox; the news had not yet reached this remote corner of south Texas. Known as the Battle of Palmito Ranch, it was won by the

❧ Goings-on at the Gulf ❧

Charro Days Fiesta, Brownsville

Confederates, who then had the distressing experience of being taken prisoner by the Union forces they had just defeated when news came that the victors in the battle had already lost the war.

At the time of the Civil War, two towns, Clarksville and Bagdad, stood facing one another across the mouth of the Rio Grande, but both were effectively destroyed by hurricanes a few years later. Clarksville never consisted of much more than a customs post, an observatory and a few houses made of wood salvaged from shipwrecks; but until 1865 Bagdad, on the Mexican bank, had fifteen thousand inhabitants and was described as 'the lifeblood of the South'. It had started life as a settlement known as Boca del Rio (Mouth of the River); goods were smuggled from the north across the river and then distributed to Mexican merchants from the interior. The business soon became so lucrative that Americans renamed the town Bagdad, supposedly because of its fabulous and illicit wealth. After Matamoros and Bagdad had been declared a free-trade zone in 1858, imports increased dramatically, with Bagdad now being used as a seaport, despite having no protection from the Gulf. The Civil War brought a blockade by the Union navy of all Texas Gulf ports, including Clarksville, but the Rio Grande was an international waterway and so the river traffic continued largely undisturbed by the war.

Mifflin Kenedy and Richard King (later of the King Ranch), both from Irish families by way of, respectively, Pennsylvania and New York, owned and operated steamboats under the Mexican flag, bringing cotton from east Texas, Louisiana and Arkansas down river to Matamoros, Bagdad and thence to Havana and on to Europe. The money from cotton bought guns and ammunition, food, medicine and clothes for the Confederacy. The cargoes had to be transferred by lighter to and from the seagoing ships lying off Bagdad; according to a contemporary account, sometimes as many as three hundred, from diverse countries, were to be seen offshore. Goods were also ferried across the river between Brownsville and Matamoros, until Brownsville fell (temporarily) to the Union at the end of 1863. The combination of Confederate trade (sometimes with Yankee entrepreneurs who put profit before politics) and the migration of Union sympathisers across the river to Mexico at the start of the war turned Matamoros and Bagdad into boom towns. Property values soared, an English-language newspaper was published and the population of Matamoros increased at least fourfold. By 1865, Bagdad had two-storey buildings, hotels, theatres. A contemporary map marks an abattoir and a cemetery, and a local newsletter recommends 'a marvellous balsam to cure pneumonia'.

Before the Civil War ended a French naval force had bombarded Bagdad in the name of the newly installed Emperor Maximilian, while affirming support for the Confederacy. Troops loyal to Benito Juárez retook Bagdad and Matamoros two years later in a bloody siege. A group of black Union soldiers embarking for home later left their mark when they looted Bagdad and murdered several of its citizens. In 1867, a hurricane flattened the town, but it continued as a port, with a passenger service down the coast to Tampico, until another hurricane finally ended its life in 1889. Bagdad had served no real purpose since the Civil War, and its Texan opposite number, Clarksville, was never rebuilt after the 1867 hurricane.

Over the past century numerous relics and memorabilia from the twin towns at the mouth of the river – cartridges, sabres, cutlery, gold and silver coins – have been dug from the sand. Today you are more likely to find a cache of drugs. A man from Ohio, intending to visit the grave of an ancestor who had lived in Bagdad in the 1860s, was amazed to find nothing but sand remaining. I decided to make my own way to the beach, twenty miles east of Matamoros, to have a look.

The local minibus, with seating provided by two hard, narrow benches facing one another, bumped its way out of town, heading towards the Ciudad Industrial de Matamoros (where the foreign-owned *maquiladoras*,* or assembly plants, are located). Here a few shift-workers got out at a vast, hangar-like building where they would be occupied for the next ten hours in making brushes. Towards Bagdad, the partly cultivated land turns to sandflats, then patches of water where herons and egrets loiter expectantly. When we reached the beach the bus turned south along the sand for a mile or so, past open fishing boats hauled from the water. From one of them a box of small sharks was being unloaded and packed with seaweed from the shore. To our right a row of bars stood on wooden stilts, with fishermen's shacks behind. On a February weekday no one was coming to the beach for recreation, and there was no one to board the bus back to Matamoros.

Going up the beach again, I asked the driver whether we were now heading north as far as the border. No, he said, there was nothing there, and anyway the mouth of the river was four miles away and we might get stuck in the sand. As I looked towards Texas, a haze hung over the coastline and long lines of surf rolled in from the Gulf. This was Playa Bagdad, also called Playa General Lauro Villar after a local hero of the Mexican Revolution. It had a few buildings, rows of rushy beach parasols and a raised look-out platform – and it was the nearest we would get to the site of the old town of Bagdad. But the driver agreed to wait while I got out to inspect the only permanent, hurricane-resistant structure: a statue of Christopher Columbus, pointing optimistically inland. It was put there in 1992 to mark the five hundredth anniversary of Columbus's first voyage to the New World. When I mentioned this to the bus driver he told me he didn't even know whose statue it was – though he passed it several times every day. Back in Matamoros, it was not until I got up to leave the bus that I realised how my back had suffered from the hard seat and the state of the road. I staggered down the street from the Plaza Allende to the nineteenth-century cathedral

---

* *see pages 61-65.*

which preceded Bagdad's boom period – and decided to come back another day to admire the architecture of Matamoros.

Matamoros was so named in 1826, not because of its literal meaning – Kill Moors – or any supposed Arab connection with Bagdad, but after a padre who had fought with distinction and died in Mexico's struggle for independence. At about this time, another padre, Nicolas Balli, started the building of the church, Nuestra Señora del Refugio, which was granted cathedral status in the 1950s by Pope John XXIII. It is a fine, twin-towered building, designed by a New Orleans architect and reconstructed after hurricane damage in the same French Creole style, though today's spires are rather different from the original rounded towers. Unfortunately Padre Balli died before the church was completed, but his name is perpetuated in Padre Island north of the Rio Grande. The Ballis, a German-Italian family from Strasbourg who first came to Mexico in the sixteenth century, had large landholdings on both sides of the river until the Mexican–American War. Then they decided to consolidate their position in south Texas, though sometimes facing competition from immigrants fleeing the ravages of the potato famine in Ireland. A McAllen, a Plantation Scot who had arrived from Londonderry, founded the border city which was named after him, thanks at least in part to his marriage into the Balli family which owned enough land in the Rio Grande valley to make it possible. (The family name is to be seen every day in Brownsville on the doors of Balli taxis.)

A larger influx, however, from Europe and from elsewhere in the United States, was settling on the right bank of the river. Charles Stillman lived in Matamoros, trading by ship with Connecticut and New York for twenty years before he founded the city of Brownsville at the end of the Mexican–American War. William Neale, from Sussex, set up in business as a house painter and later ran a stage between Boca del Rio (Bagdad) and Matamoros before crossing the river to make a name for himself in Brownsville. As a Confederate officer, he commuted between the two towns during the Civil War. At the time of the Mexican–American War, Irishmen who had turned up in Texas having just been forced out of their country by the famine for which they blamed the English, were more inclined to join their Catholic comrades south of the river. Business links between Matamoros and New Orleans also brought French families to the Rio Grande, but they continued to send their children back to Louisiana for a French education. The architectural influence of the French Quarter of New Orleans can still be seen in the long wrought-iron balconies of some of Matamoros's houses as well as in the French Creole cathedral. In a street near the international bridge, I came across another reminder of Matamoros's former elegance: a Greek Revival house flanked by cypresses and standing between two miserable, flat-topped blocks of concrete.

In the 1880s an Englishman called Meliton Cross built a house in Matamoros which must be one of the strangest architectural survivals of any Mexican border town. It is wonderfully out of place – brick-built and painted dark red, with verandahs, rounded lintels over shuttered windows, a dormer window in the slate roof, elaborate eaves and, most remarkable of all in Mexico, red-brick chimneys. Casa Cross was restored in 1992 by a Mexican enthusiast, Filemon Garza, and one hopes that funds remain available to maintain the house. When I saw it in 2000 the shutters were in need of attention.

Until the Mexican–American War, Matamoros was so cosmopolitan that its newspapers – in particular *El Correo del Rio Grande* – were published in English and French as well as Spanish. When Zachary Taylor set up his headquarters in 1846 at Fort Brown, across the river from Matamoros, he authorised the publication of two news-sheets, *American Flag* and, in Matamoros, *Reveille*, whose purpose was to promote the cause of the United States – confirming its frontier at the Rio Grande, if not farther south. Inevitably, after two years of war and the founding of the town of Brownsville on the north bank, 'Anglo' residents moved across the river. But their business and personal connections with Mexican Matamoros continued, and are retained to this day. It might have been politically prudent to live on one side of the river or the other, but the enemies of 1846–8 were to become allies again little more than a decade later, against the hated Yankees of the north. The Yankee General Ulysses S. Grant and the Confederate General Robert E. Lee, on the other hand, having both been billeted at Fort Brown and then having fought together in Mexico, at Cerro Gordo and Chapultepec, were obliged to slog it out in the subsequent war of attrition and slaughter 'between the states'. Mifflin Kenedy and Richard King, who had properties in both Brownsville and Matamoros while they ran their riverboat company, captained the boats that took Zachary Taylor's army up to Camargo in 1846, and after that war made money transporting Americans heading to California for the Gold Rush. From the east coast they came by ship to Port Isabel, thence by river from Brownsville as far as they could go (Camargo or Mier), across country to Mazatlan and up the Gulf of California to Hermosillo. It was a much shorter and less expensive route than going round Cape Horn.

Operating their boats on behalf of the Confederacy during the Civil War, Kenedy and King were friends also to the merchant class on both sides of the river and to the imperialist supporters of Maximilian. A no less significant figure of the time was the Mexican Juan Cortina, whose influence also straddled the border. He backed the Juáristas in Mexico's civil war, seeking the restoration of Benito Juárez as president, the Union forces in America's Civil War and the oppressed Mexican Americans of Brownsville. Perhaps because he spent much of his time rustling cattle and making trouble on the Texas bank of the river, and because his mother had a ranch there, Cortina's Brownsville Raid of 1859 was not classified as an invasion of US territory in the same way that Pancho Villa's border raid on Columbus, New Mexico would be in 1916. But President Wilson was more edgy about international relations and the threat of war in 1916 than was President Buchanan who, in 1859, had the threat of an internal war to worry about.

In Brownsville, where he held a number of local government officials in his power, Cortina was almost literally a law unto himself. When he was indicted for robbery or assault, no one dared arrest him, and he merely withdrew across the border for a while. (There was no extradition treaty between Mexico and the United States.) He reasoned that the best way to consolidate his political power in Brownsville was to lead an armed raid on the town. And so, at dawn on 28 September, he took two hundred men with him across the river, occupied Fort Brown, raised the Mexican flag, released prisoners from the county jail and gave them arms. He kept the town under siege for three days until regular Mexican troops came from Matamoros to defuse the situation, persuading Cortina to withdraw across the river. Mifflin Kenedy organised a local militia to guard against his return; when Cortina renewed his siege of Brownsville, he advanced to within a few hundred yards of the town square. The Governor of Texas sent in a posse of Texas Rangers to help restore order in the delta, and US troops were returned to Fort Brown, almost two months after its occupation by Cortina's band of irregulars. One of the Rangers' commanders, Major 'Rip' Ford (he was responsible for recording the deaths of US troops during the Mexican–American War, writing RIP beside each name), visited Cortina's mother at her ranch and offered her protection. He then pursued his quarry up river as far as Rio Grande City, where sixty of Cortina's men were ambushed and killed, though Cortina himself managed to escape by swimming his horse across the river. Ford later took his Rangers into Mexico, risking an international incident, which may well have been his intention. Ford was a colourful figure: originally from South Carolina, he had been a teacher, lawyer and playwright. As a Confederate officer, he played a significant part in the redundant Battle of Palmito Ranch after the Confederates had surrendered. He had agitated for Matamoros to be a free-trade zone, and after the war he went to Mexico to fight for the Juáristas, finding himself alongside his old enemy, Juan Cortina. Cortina made himself Governor of Tamaulipas, but on the left bank he continued cattle rustling, selling the American-branded animals to Cuba via Bagdad. Having served as mayor of Matamoros a few years later, he hoped to settle with his family in Brownsville. But Porfirio Díaz, and his influential supporters in Brownsville (Díaz had stayed there the year before he became president), wanted Cortina removed from the valley; and it was only thanks to the intercession of Rip Ford that Cortina escaped a firing squad. He spent the rest of his life under house arrest in Mexico City; but he is not forgotten in Brownsville or in Matamoros. In Matamoros's Fort Casamata museum he is commemorated as a doughty fighter against 'the barbarians, North Americans, French and Imperialists' – though he quite often had North Americans on his side.

The careers of Cortina and Ford provide a good illustration of the close historical links between the two border towns, the communication and the intercourse which have always taken place across this narrow river boundary. Nowhere else along the border, except in Laredo and Nuevo Laredo, do the two adjacent communities seem to have such a mutual understanding based on their shared past. Not only did a Rio Grande Republic come briefly into being in Laredo in 1840 but, ten years later, something similar was planned by a federalist faction which was active farther down river, on the right bank between Camargo and Matamoros, and for a time the plans included Rip Ford.

Yolanda González, a tutor at the University of Texas at Brownsville, is one of the many Mexican Texans who, one supposes, might favour some sort of autonomous Rio Grande territory. She tends to speak of Matamoros/Brownsville as one place. 'We are all part of the same community,' she told me. 'I go to Matamoros almost every week to visit my relatives – there are many families with property on both sides of the river.

'I don't look upon the river as a frontier between two separate countries. Don't forget, we are all descended from European stock. The frontier is supposed to keep the Mexicans out, but the Border Patrol has only a limited effect. And why should we worry about this so-called illegal immigration – America is a nation of immigrants, after all. However, we have to obey the regulations. My husband is a Mexican who is awaiting US citizenship. Meanwhile he has a permit to work here in Brownsville.'

Señora González is descended from the Salinas family which owned the land on which Zachary Taylor established his headquarters (afterwards known as Fort Brown) and provoked Mexico to war in 1846. She says, not entirely seriously, that she is still awaiting compensation for the land grab, but is pleased that much of the old family land now belongs to the University of Texas. She looked across to Brownsville's imposing Catholic cathedral, commenting again on the interdependence of the two communities, and made the point that other denominations were also represented in both towns. Presbyterians, Quakers and Methodists established their churches, and schools, in Brownsville soon after its founding in 1848; and they expanded across the river not many years later. Matamoros had the first Presbyterian church in northern Mexico, and from there the mission penetrated into the interior. The Baptist church, oddly enough, began its mission in Matamoros, and did not cross to Brownsville until the early years of the twentieth century.

At midday on a Sunday I found a full house, with scarcely any standing room, to celebrate mass at the Cathedral of the Immaculate Conception, which looks from the outside not unlike an English parish church of the sixteenth century. Its rectory has provided sanctuary for priests fleeing various Mexican revolutions and upheavals over the past hundred and fifty years. There is a tradition of Brownsville giving refuge to victims of violent goings-on across the border. When, in 1915, a contingent of followers of Pancho Villa laid siege to Matamoros, their wounded were tended by residents of Brownsville – in spite of the wild shooting which resulted in several houses and people in Brownsville being hit from the other side of the river.

The fortunes of the twin cities have also been historically interdependent, having a seesaw effect. An economic boom in one has usually depressed the other, whether due to conditions of trade between the two countries or movements of population. Divisions and hostilities developed, too, after the Mexican–American War when Brownsville was founded initially by and for Anglos, and the Hispanics were the underdogs (and so championed by Juan Cortina). There was an element of racism for some years which was not present further up river in Laredo, where the population was always almost entirely Hispanic. But today Brownsville is about eighty per cent Hispanic and, more importantly, an equivalent proportion of its public offices is held by Mexican Americans who, one Anglo resident of Brownsville told me, are often more public-spirited and conscientious than Anglo public servants and more persistent when it comes to getting federal aid for south Texas.

What amounts to a Mexican fiesta takes place very year in Brownsville during the last week of February. It has been compared to Mardi Gras and is described as a bi-cultural festival, but it is in fact a celebration of the Mexican heritage of the twin cities. Called Charro Days (*charro* is Spanish for cowboy, though the word also means an ill-mannered person), the four-day fiesta has been held annually since 1938. It traditionally starts with a *grito* (a cry: the Mexican national anthem urges 'Mexicanos, al Grito de Guerra') and continues with parades in Mexican costume, *mariachi* bands and taco-eating contests. The mayors of Brownsville and Matamoros meet in the middle of the Gateway International Bridge to exchange gifts and mouth platitudes about the Rio Grande uniting instead of dividing the two cities. At the ceremony in 2000, the playing of 'The Star-Spangled Banner' was drowned by catcalls for a male Mexican soap-opera star who was invited on to the bridge as celebrity guest and given an unofficial award as El Galan del Año (Hunk of the Year).

One evening I dropped in on a Baile Ranchero at the Jacob Brown Auditorium, commemorating the Major Brown who was killed by Mexicans in 1846 while defending the fort and had the city of Brownsville named after him. A plaque outside the hall refers to the century of peace which the two republics have enjoyed, and the harmony and understanding which exist among the 'two nations on the Rio Grande'. On this night it was easier to think of them as one nation: the Orquesta Barbosa y Cia from Monterrey in Nuevo León was playing as Brownsville's inhabitants flocked into the auditorium in their Mexican fancy dress. Many of the ladies were wearing traditional black with gold-leaf embroidery, while the men sported black *charro* trousers, Emiliano Zapata style, with silver buttons down the outside seams. Most of them, of course, had Mexican blood and felt entirely at home at a Mexican evening. Outside, across the road and alongside the international bridge, the German shepherd dogs of the US Border Patrol were barking in their compound. I wondered if they were irritated by the uniquely Mexican *mariachi* music – or possibly anxious to get out and sniff for some smuggled cocaine or wetback flesh.

Saturday was the day of the Grand International Parade. The procession included floats and bands from both Matamoros and Brownsville: they started in the main shopping street and then some turned right through the US border checkpoint and over the bridge to Mexico. It was certainly an eclectic parade, led by four Mexicans on horseback. They were carrying the flags of Mexico and the United States, so presumably two were Mexican Americans. But they all had moustaches, wore sombreros and brandished swords. After them came the bands, the dancers on decorated floats, Mexican children dressed up in traditional costume and perched on the back of pick-up trucks. There was a life-size model of a matador and bull, a trio of Vietnam veterans in combat uniform and a few elderly 'winter Texans' (those annual visitors from the Midwest and Canada) waving to the crowds. The best reception was accorded to a Matamoros school band – trumpets, saxophones, clarinets – giving a spirited rendering of 'La Cucaracha'. It was a bizarre sight to watch this colourful procession, for one day a year excused the international tolls, making its way past the duty-free shops, the *casas de cambio* and the police and border guards to walk or drive over the river to continue the Fiestas del Charro in Mexico. On one truck a woman in a decorative cowgirl outfit with leather tassels was talking into a mobile telephone.

The honouring of Mr Amigo is one of the highlights of the festival, a title given to a person (always a Mexican) judged to have made a major contribution to international friendship and mutual understanding between the two countries. The winner for Charro Days 2000 was unusual on two counts: Mr Amigo was a woman, and she failed to turn up to receive her award. The problem was that while Silvia Pinal, a Mexican actress, may have done great work in promoting relations between Mexico and the United States, she had not been so successful in her relations with the Mexican government, which had issued a warrant for her arrest on charges of fraud and tax evasion. So she was represented by her two daughters, one of whom was considered an acceptable substitute as she had once appeared naked in *Playboy* magazine. The other got married during the festivities; having been conveyed over the bridge to Matamoros as part of the parade, she promptly drove back to the United States for a wedding party at the Holiday Inn at Fort Brown. At the nearby Sombrero Festival in Washington Park a jalapeño pepper eating contest was being watched by bemused children dressed in the colours (red, white and green) of the Mexican flag.

Reflecting an imbalance found between other border towns, the population of the Mexican twin, Matamoros, is several times larger than Brownsville's due in part to the number of people, approaching one hundred thousand in 2000, who now work in the Matamoros *maquiladoras*. Brownsville's commercial importance derives from its port, constructed in the 1930s at the end of a ship channel seventeen miles from the Gulf of Mexico. Twenty years later it was the largest cotton port in the United States, with the great majority of the cotton coming from Mexico. By the mid-1990s the cotton trade through Brownsville had ended; so had the tropical fruit business and the number of shrimp boats had halved. The shrimp trawling industry is still thriving (around fifteen million pounds weight of what the English call prawns are landed each year in Brownsville), but when Mexico extended its territorial waters to two hundred miles, the boats were excluded from their lucrative fishing grounds in the Gulf of Campeche across to the Yucatán peninsula. Today the port's principal cargo, unloaded from European as well as American ships and bound for Mexico, is steel (which Mexico also exports). On any day, hundreds of steel coils, bars and plates can be seen on the quays awaiting transportation to Mexico, where most are destined for the car-construction industry. What is surprising about a port having eighty per cent of its trade with Mexico is that in 2000 no international bridge had been built to link the port, which is only three miles north of the Rio Grande, directly with Mexico, bypassing Matamoros and giving much faster access to and from the *maquiladoras* and the main road south. Truck and rail traffic has to go instead through the conurbations of Brownsville and Matamoros. Though proposals for a new route had been discussed, on and off, for at least forty years, agreement between the US and Mexican governments had still not been reached in 2000. Objections had been raised by wildlife conservationists concerned for the survival of two endangered species of wild cat, the ocelot and the jaguarundi, living in the river valley. But the port

✢ Goings-on at the Gulf ✢

authorities remained optimistic that a bridge, with roads and railtrack, would be built in the first decade of this century.

The railways came late to Brownsville/Matamoros. Apart from a short rail link between Port Isabel and Brownsville, begun in 1872, no railway connecting Mexico via Brownsville to the rest of Texas was opened until the first years of the twentieth century (when the last riverboat ceased to run on the Rio Grande). There is no passenger rail service in the Rio Grande valley today, but the freight trains trundle frequently across the river, sometimes pulling as many as a hundred wagons or boxcars. One day I stood by the rail bridge watching as a long train with the name of Union Pacific on its boxcars took about ten minutes to pass, heading slowly north to San Antonio. I asked a Mexican–American Border Patrol guard what was being carried. 'Steel, I guess, and manufactured goods too,' he said. 'And maybe a few wetbacks.' He didn't seem too concerned at this possibility, explaining to me how immigrants would often hide in the boxcars, or hang on underneath them, as they crossed into the United States. Sometimes they are found in the boxcars having died of heat exhaustion; others break arms and legs jumping on to and off the trains. But this train was not going to be searched here at the border; perhaps it would be stopped at a checkpoint further up the line. There was more activity to be observed when I walked back to the Gateway road bridge. A Border Patrol vehicle was speeding along the riverbank, though no fugitive was in sight, raising clouds of dust which temporarily obscured the eyesore sign of the Holiday Inn.

Barry Horn, director of the local symphony orchestra, invited me to inspect the international border from his farm which runs down to the Rio Grande a few miles west of town. His family grows sorghum (from which molasses is made) almost to the riverbank; on the other side was another field planted with sorghum, yet in forty years the Horns had never had any contact with their Mexican neighbour. In the distance, a factory was visible: a chemical plant, I was told, which was highly toxic and potentially dangerous. But there was nothing much that anyone in south Texas could do about it.

On the levee, parallel to and a hundred yards back from the river, a Border Patrol agent was sitting at the wheel of his Ford Expedition, looking south through his binoculars. It was a bright early spring afternoon and the visibility was good. No *indocumentados* were likely to make the crossing in this open country before dark.

Agent Jim Hays, a Texan from Orange, on the border with Louisiana, had been patrolling this stretch for several weeks. The night before, he had caught a party of five Mexicans, including two women; one escaped back across the river.

'It was probably a coyote [the courier who is paid to escort immigrants across the border] that got away,' Agent Hays told me. 'He ran back as soon as he saw the vehicle and jumped into the water. The others didn't give any trouble – they are usually pretty passive when they know they're going to be arrested.'

Once caught, an illegal immigrant is taken to Brownsville for fingerprinting, then checked with the computer to discover whether and where he has crossed before. Unless he has a long history of previous attempts, he will simply be deported – taken back across the bridge and dumped in Matamoros.

'We normally allow them up to fifteen "hits" before taking them to court,' Agent Hays said. 'It depends how they behave in custody and who's on duty at the station. A judge will probably only detain them for a few days anyway.' (But if they get as far as Houston, and come before the courts charged with another offence under Texas law, they may be imprisoned for up to seven years.)

Agent Hays's AOR (area of responsibility) does not extend for more than half a mile of riverbank. His is one of fifty-two vehicles patrolling twenty-five miles. That is a lot of vehicles, but he readily concedes that it is not an efficient use of resources. They probably don't catch more than fifty per cent of illegal immigrants. While Border Patrol agents have authority to drive over private land up to twenty-five miles from the border, they do not pursue their quarry on foot.

'They only have to get as far as that brush over there and they've escaped us,' Agent Hays explained, 'though, of course, they may be picked up later, farther north.'

'I'm sure glad you don't chase them into that thicket and disturb the wildlife,' said Barry Horn. 'We've got bobcats and nutria in there' – he pointed to his wood, which ran back to the edge of his property – 'also armadillos and coyotes – mostly the four-legged variety, I'm glad to say.'

The conversation was entirely friendly, but Mr Horn told me later that if he were ever to apprehend an immigrant on his land, he would not turn him in. This sympathy for the plight of Mexicans driven by intolerable economic conditions to seek work in the USA may be shared by a number of riverine Texan farmers in the Rio Grande valley, many of whom are of Mexican origin; but it is by no means general. In Arizona and New Mexico, ranchers are more likely to shoot at immigrants found on their land and then hand them over to the Border Patrol. The attitudes of agents towards immigrants vary widely but are often characterised by racial and physical abuse. The Border Patrol's spokesman in Brownsville said their aim was to deal with all immigrants 'in a compassionate and generous manner' – which was a generous way of putting it; but the aim is not often achieved. Agent Hays is probably fairly typical of Anglo Texans: he had never been to Mexico, nor had he any real interest in going. But he was clearly sympathetic towards a woman he had caught recently, who with her husband had come from Veracruz, where she had left her three children, hoping to get a job but having no idea where she would go to find one.

❋ Goings-on at the Gulf ❋

The strong Border Patrol presence in this area had resulted in fewer arrests, which indicated nothing more than that fewer crossings were being made in the Brownsville sector. The immigrant problem had merely moved up river, where over the same period the number of apprehensions had increased. The immigrant grapevine had also clearly passed the word that Brownsville had been given a lot of new technology to make the Border Patrol's job more effective. On the roof of Brownsville's tallest building – which is not a hotel or office block, but the Villa del Sol nursing home, built at the instigation of a rabbi – a long-range infra-red telescope can spot prospective immigrants at night on the Mexican bank of the river as they prepare to cross. It sounds almost like cheating. In their vehicles some agents have infra-red thermal imaging systems which enable them to locate movements in darkness. They are supplied with night-vision goggles and have sensors buried in the ground along the riverbank. Searchlights are erected on top of the levee.

As we waited in the field at dusk, duck flew overhead and dogs were barking in Mexico. Not knowing if we would see an unfortunate Mexican come running out of the scrub at the top of the steep riverbank, I was suddenly put in mind of duck-flighting at home. You waited hopefully in the gathering gloom, but you never quite knew whether they were going to come in. We got talking about the recent announcement from America's largest labour union, AFL–CIO, that it was seeking an amnesty for undocumented foreign workers. This was an astonishing turnabout for an organisation which until then had been consistently opposed to immigrant labour. AFL–CIO had been largely instrumental in getting sanctions imposed on employers with illegal immigrants on their payrolls. At the same time, in early 2000, the US Federal Reserve chairman, Alan Greenspan, said the only answer to current labour shortages in the USA was to increase immigration quotas before the labour market showed signs of inflationary pressure. And there was a proposal to revive the concept of the *bracero* (guest-worker) programme for Mexicans, which was established during the Second World War and did not end until 1964. I asked Agent Hays about the possible loosening of restrictions on immigrant labour.

'If there is an amnesty, or if seasonal visas are granted, it will only encourage more people to cross illegally,' he said. 'As long as Mexico fails to provide the hope of a better future, they will keep coming. And not only from Mexico – but from El Salvador, Guatemala, Honduras. There are already more than ten million Hispanics living in California. I read somewhere that within fifty years the United States will cease to be a predominantly white country.'

It was something to ponder as Agent Hays and I parted, soon after dark. No *indocumentados* had yet been spotted as he walked down to the river to inspect the likely landings, the places where crossings are often made. His footfalls were drowned by the insistent calling of crickets.

Agent Hays had not arrested any drug-smugglers on his beat. He recalled the 'wild times' he had had when stationed up at El Paso, and then on the Arizona border, where the drugs traffic was heavier; but down here he was dealing only with economic migrants. This could mean that the drugs traffic had moved up river, or that the smugglers were crossing the river undetected. Both explanations were likely: those carrying drugs, known in Border Patrol language as backpackers, are smarter than the *mojados*, who may be dumped by their coyotes at the first sign of trouble. Drugs seizures are more likely to be made at road checkpoints farther north. A week after I left the Rio Grande, evidence of the power of the drugs barons in Matamoros was macabrely provided when a Border Patrol agent went to investigate a bundle which had been carried across the river and left on the Texas bank. It contained the body of a Mexican journalist, known in Matamoros for his coverage of the drugs trade in the newspaper *La Opinion*, who had been shot in the back of the head. Drugs-related crime on the border produces from the

Mexican public little more than a shrug of the shoulders; and it rarely attracts moral censure. A local song, 'Fronteras de Tamaulipas', tells the story, without any condemnation, of a *contrabandista* who shoots dead a senior customs official for refusing to accept his bribe, then fords the river to Texas. The last verse begs Matamoros not to change, to remain a city of violence and disorder, 'the haven of my desire':

> Matamoros, Tamaulipas,
> nunca dejas de ser
> la ciudad mas bullanguera,
> el puerto de mi querer.

Desirable or not, the endemic violence may help to explain why a recent mayor of Matamoros chose to live in Brownsville – judging that it might be safer to reside in a different country from the one in which he carried out his public duties. It may appear inconceivable to an outsider, but on this Tex–Mex border things are different.

Chapter Three

Mexican Texas

FROM THE Texas border town of Hidalgo across the Rio Grande to Reynosa, the river is less than a hundred yards wide. The last shop on the American side offers not watches and sunglasses but relojes y lentes para sol. As soon as you have crossed the bridge into Mexico, you are greeted by hoardings in English, advertising medical and dental services. 'Prevenitive [sic] Medicine' – 'Alternative to Bypass Surgery' – 'Oxidative Therapy' – 'Doctors Center, Great Prices!'. A Dental Plaza displays a red poster outside, showing two rows of teeth covered with braces made of silver foil. An orthodontist offers 'Root Canal $69, Porcelain Crowns $99'. Back in the United States large posters proclaim the advantages of attending the Valley Regional Health Center. But a lot of 'winter Texans' prefer a cheaper health service – not to mention cheaper alcohol – south of the border.

I am not sure whether I would choose to have root-canal treatment in a Third World country. First impressions of Reynosa were not favourable: the wind was blowing dust and rubbish from a site where buildings were being demolished; plaster was peeling from the walls of the Doctors Center. I passed an unappealing hotel next to one of the town's many car-repair shops, and a branch of Citibank which had closed its doors, seemingly for good. A guidebook recommended the craft markets and several restaurants, but the swirling dust drove me back across the bridge. That evening I looked up Graham Greene's short story, 'Across the Bridge', set in a Mexican border town on the Rio

Grande in the 1930s. An American plain-clothes policeman was expecting to find 'life' on the other side. 'You read things about Mexico,' he said. But instead he found 'wide mud streets where the nocturnal rain lay in pools, and mangy dogs, smells and cockroaches in his bedroom'. It hasn't changed that much.

Adjoining Hidalgo is McAllen, named after a Plantation Scot who, through his marriage to a member of the Balli family, acquired some two hundred thousand acres in the valley. I met up with his great-grandson, James McAllen, who today has fifty thousand acres and around two thousand head of cattle. He was complaining of the shortage of cowboys.

'The United States education system does not raise people to be cowboys. Ranchers still need cowboys and Mexicans are ideal for the job. But getting permission to bring over and employ a Mexican takes so much time and bureaucracy.

'I could get a wetback tomorrow, but if he's caught not only will he be deported – I could face a large fine and imprisonment.'

A neighbour had a similar problem on his vegetable farm, because only Mexicans will pick the okra, which has nasty little spines and is inclined to give you a rash. The local Texans, he said, would rather 'sit around on food stamps'. The tradition for years has been for Mexicans to slip across the river to do the 'stoop labour', picking peppers, squash, cucumbers, as well as okra, then return home with their earnings. For some of the time, at least, the Border Patrol turns a blind eye because these workers are not heading north. But the economy of the Rio Grande valley is not so dependent on its soil any more. The famous freeze of 1983 put paid to a large part of the palm tree and citrus fruit industry, and in the past two decades a winter tourism industry has developed for an area which in January, February and March is often warmer than Florida.

For the fruit, vegetable and sugar-cane farmers who remain in business, times have become hard. A grapefruit grower, Jimmy Steidinger, with two hundred acres near McAllen, was already suffering because of NAFTA, the North American Free Trade Agreement, which allowed Mexican farmers to export their crops free of tariffs. Now he was short of water because Mexico was in breach of its treaty obligations by refusing to release the stuff from its Rio Grande tributaries and from reservoirs up river; and the problem was exacerbated by several years of drought. At the turn of the century Mr Steidinger had to face the prospect of Mexico increasing its market share, which already exceeded forty per cent of all the fresh fruit and vegetables sold in North America. Since Mexico already owed the south Texas farmers several billion gallons of water, their best bet for the future was thought to be a dam in the lower river valley.

All south Texas border towns are relatively run-down – they are among the poorest metropolitan areas in the USA – due to the large unskilled labour pool. It consists mainly of immigrants, many of whom first crossed the river at the time of the *bracero*, or guest-worker, programme of the 1940s–60s. (*Braceros* work with their *brazos*, arms, but wealthy Mexicans came too during this time, investing their money in condominiums on South Padre Island.) With agriculture in decline today, there is evidence of real depression in some rural towns. When I passed through Falfurrias, halfway to Alice on the San Antonio road, it seemed that almost every building was unoccupied, boarded-up or semi-derelict. In Hidalgo County, between Edinburg and the Rio Grande, there are almost a thousand *colonias*, most of them unsignposted and with unpaved roads, giving some form of insanitary accommodation to hundreds of thousands of Spanish-speaking residents. Both poverty and polio have still to be eradicated in the valley – probably the only place in the USA where the disease is still found – and the incidence of hepatitis A in Hidalgo County at the end of the century was four times higher than in the rest of Texas. The rate of population increase south of the border – a billion Mexicans by the year 2100 have been estimated – is such that gloomy Malthusian predictions are heard, with the border region the first to be affected.

Perhaps the most uplifting sight in the valley is the huge representation of Christ, in coloured glass and ceramic chips, on one of the exterior walls of the Church of La Virgen de San Juan del Valle, outside McAllen. The work of an Italian, it shows Christ blue-robed in the clouds, looking down on the Rio Grande winding its way through the fertile fields of the valley. In the garden on the other side of the church is a white statue of the kneeling Rachel, inscribed 'In Remembrance of Babies Robbed of Their Birth'. A little way behind her, standing above Highway 83, there is a prominent PAWN sign, bearing witness to a more pervasive form of American robbery. The church was built to replace its predecessor on the site which was destroyed in 1954 when a plane deliberately crashed into it. Did the pilot, I wondered, bear some grudge against the Catholic Church? Was he perhaps making a statement in favour of women priests or of moderating the insistence on priestly celibacy? I asked a gardener, who spoke no English. 'Loco,' he said, shrugging his shoulders and smiling.

San Juan is one of several towns along Highway 83 – Pharr, Weslaco, Donna, Harlingen, San Benito – to have promoted themselves in recent years as resorts for winter tourism. But at least one of them, Donna, also has its darker side. It is said that witchcraft is practised there – not by the local *curandero*, or healer, but by those, often connected with drug-smuggling, who indulge in blood sacrifices and believe they receive supernatural protection through black-magic rituals.

One police raid in 1989 uncovered a blood-stained altar and a cauldron containing human remains. The rituals, apparently of Caribbean origin, may involve ingesting human brains and seminal fluid. For this purpose bright, white, athletic types are more in demand than impoverished Hispanics. Not long ago a good-looking, fair-haired student from Houston, who had been picked up on the Matamoros–Reynosa highway, became a sacrificial victim.

It was a few miles south of Donna, across the river and along Carretera 2, east of Reynosa, that I visited a *maquiladora* for the first time. This has been the largest growing industry on the border since it was started in Ciudad Juárez in 1965. The idea of the Border Industrialization Program was that Mexico would allow American companies to assemble pre-manufactured components (from vehicle airbags to sweatshirts) in Mexico, using cheap local labour to help alleviate unemployment along the border. The parts, together with capital equipment and machinery, were permitted to be brought into Mexico duty-free, and when the finished products were exported to the United States, duty would be payable only on the value added during the assembly process. For the Mexican border areas the main benefit, apart from jobs, was the acquisition of know-how, which could later be used to establish competing all-Mexican companies. After this arrangement had continued for about thirty years, the Mexican government started talking about the need for the foreign companies to make a proper fiscal contribution. A tax on the value of foreign assets (*maquila* plant and machinery) was expected to be introduced after 2002. Since the coming of NAFTA in 1994, foreign companies from countries outside the free-trade area, mainly Korea, Japan and China, have been obliged to negotiate tariffs for the production materials which they bring in to the *maquilas*.

According to a booklet on the Border Industrialization Program issued in 1971, women are better suited to *maquila* work than men, because 'from their earliest conditioning, [they] show respect and obedience to persons in authority, especially men. The women follow orders willingly, accept change and adjustments easily, and are considered less demanding.' Not much prospect here of female emancipation or equal rights for women. It is certainly the case that most *maquila* workers (around seventy-five per cent) are women; as in other Third

World countries, they traditionally do the jobs which may be mind-numbingly repetitive, and involve eye strain and other health hazards. They are supposedly better than men at doing the fiddly fingerwork often required in the *maquiladoras*: sewing sweatshirts, assembling tiny electronic circuitry, setting rivets, fixing washers. I was told that at one company, which puts together cassette tapes, each worker will, during an eight-hour shift, apply 48,000 dabs of glue to the cassette casings. Women are also more suitable, it is said, for work in the *maquila* environment where there is little prospect of advancement. A relatively quick turnover of employees is not discouraged by employers concerned that workers with any length of service might start demanding and exercising rights which have been denied them.

Productivity in the *maquiladoras* has allegedly been stepped up since 1994, without any consequent increase in benefits paid to employees. Real wages have in fact fallen and overtime, often treated as obligatory, is inadequately rewarded. Employers have been accused of causing undue stress to their workforce through the pace of production and the sexual harassment to which many are subjected by their supervisors. Many companies are said to enforce the practice of regular pregnancy testing so that they can lay off their pregnant workers before they are required to pay them maternity benefit. Independent unions have been discouraged and suppressed in favour of official union organisations, such as the Confederación de Trabajadores Mexicanos, which are more amenable to management and may take up to five per cent of an employee's wages in union dues. At the turn of the century, many *maquiladoras*, especially those involving a process with a high proportion of unskilled labour, were moving south, to Torreon, San Luis Potosí and as far as Yucatán. These employees' earnings would at least go into the Mexican economy, rather than be spent in the USA, as happens on the border. But earnings in interior Mexico might be forty percent lower.

❊ Mexican Texas ❊

Lower Rio Grande Valley

Stories about the border *maquiladoras* also tell of their effects on those living in the vicinity. Mexican babies have been born with brain disorders because mercury from the *maquiladoras* has got into the water. Toxic wastes are dumped close to workers' neighbourhoods or in the Rio Grande by companies confident that Mexico has neither the will nor the technology to regulate them. Allegations have also been made that US firms are illegal employers of child labour. I put these points to Javier Ledesma, director of operations at Invacare Mexico (Invamex), which assembles invalid chairs at an industrial park off the highway between Reynosa and Rio Bravo. He is also a director of the Maquiladora Association.

'There may once have been some bad eggs among the *maquilas*,' he said. 'But today it is not the foreign companies which ignore the regulations – not on this stretch of the border anyway. We are subject to very strict Mexican environmental regulations – much stricter than in the USA – which we cannot afford to ignore. There are no toxic smoke emissions here, no dumping of chemicals in the water.'

At Invamex, the 700-strong labour force works in a clean, spacious and air-conditioned environment – quite a contrast to their living conditions, which in most cases are cramped, dirty, hot and without sanitation or electricity. The average wage is only $1 per hour (across the border it would be more than $6), but with free cafeteria and free transport from and to their *colonias*, it is arguably equivalent to something nearer $2. Under Mexican law, fourteen-year-olds may be employed if their parents are suffering hardship and give permission. Mr Ledesma denied that any American company would flout this law.

I had had some trouble getting into Invamex. A non-US citizen is required by Mexican bureaucracy to have a written invitation from the *maquiladora*, then to hand over $20 at the border in exchange for an authorised visitor's permit which, of course, it takes an official more than a few minutes to issue. Once inside the assembly plant, however, you discover that it is connected to the US telephone system and not discernibly on Mexican soil.

The wheelchair parts used to come from the USA, but all of them – steel spars, wheels, upholstery – are now made in Mexico. There is no sense of sweated labour at Invamex: the overall impression is of good working space and light, without offensive fumes or dust, even in the welding areas. Of course I may have been shown a model *maquila*, one reserved for outside visitors and quite different from the much larger plants. There were allegations made against the *maquiladoras* that I was unable to check. But the evidence of Invamex certainly cleared up a few misconceptions.

In 2000, there were 135 *maquiladoras* in the Reynosa area, employing more than one hundred thousand people. They either buy their houses for cash, or build them on waste ground with corrugated-iron sheets. Their com-panies may assist a few senior employees in purchasing a house, but they generally do little or nothing to help provide paved roads, water and sewage systems in the *colonias* where their workers live. On the way back to Reynosa, we passed a sprawl of miserable shacks along the canal. Rubbish was strewn everywhere, and elderly men were driving horse-drawn carts. My driver, a *maquila* operative, said the people of this *colonia* would be earning no more than $4 a day, Mexico's legal minimum. A few hundred yards farther on, there was a private school charging the more affluent Reynosans – enriched through corruption linked to drug-dealing? – fees of $100 a month. The violence and the drugs were getting worse, the driver said, but it was not Reynosans who were responsible. It was because too many undesirables were coming to the border to look for work. So were the *maquilas* to blame? I asked. No, no, he said, and then, mysteriously, as he dropped me off at the international bridge, 'the trouble is because they're all coming from Veracruz.'

Mexican Texas

A unique US border crossing is to be found a little way upriver, at Los Ebanos, where a ferry is pulled between America and Mexico by T-shirted, peak-capped Mexicans heaving on a rope which spans the Rio Grande. Nothing much has happened in the past two centuries to alter the pace and peace of this crossing, though the wind that blows from Texas will sometimes make the pulling job a lot harder. One day a car was blown, or it may have slipped or rolled, into the river, drowning four ladies on their way to a wedding. On the flat barge three vehicles are conveyed at a time, greeted as they reach the American shore by four officers of US Customs and a detention building. A notice of risible *faux-naïveté* observes that this crossing was used in the past for smuggling; the present drug-smuggling, which is endemic on this stretch of the river, does not rate a mention. There is plenty of tree and shrub cover on both sides, and shacks in the ebony woods for hiding contraband in transit. But no wealth seems to have come to this run-down settlement, nor to its Mexican neighbour, which changed its name in the 1960s from San Miguel de Camargo to Díaz Ordaz, the name of the then president. This scarcely subtle attempt to curry favour and attract federal funds did not work; the president never came to the village named after him and its poverty was never alleviated.

However, the Mexican town called Camargo, a few miles north in Tamaulipas, has more to offer. As the first place by the river to be settled by the Spanish in the eighteenth century, Camargo has a handsome old church and square. It was mid-morning and a dark-suited man was having his shoes polished before attending a funeral in the Iglesia de Santa Ana. Old men were seated on benches, in shirt-sleeves and wearing stetsons (there was not a sombrero to be seen). One old man, similarly dressed, was sweeping the cobbles of the plaza outside the Palacio Municipal. In a country whose streets are frequently dirty and foul-smelling, it is odd to find so many employed as street-sweepers. On the bridge between Camargo and Rio Grande City, I watched a man diligently sweeping rubbish and dust towards a gutter, but most of it blew away before it got there. Lorries from the Mexican interior carrying building blocks to the United States were wished 'Feliz Viaje' by a sign as they left Mexico, but they faced a near-stationary queue for an hour or more on the bridge (the river is wider here than farther downstream) before they could resume their journey with any *felicidad*. This bridge, a Sri Chinmoy peace bridge according to a plaque, 'unites Mexico and the US [and] is officially dedicated to the goals of peace and goodwill amongst peoples and nations... It joins over two hundred such sites dedicated to peace worldwide.' Which is all very admirable; but what about prosperity?

The nineteenth-century president, Benito Juárez, is quoted on another plaque on the bridge: 'Among individuals as among nations, respect towards others' rights is peace.' Respect towards others' supposed rights to live where they want – for Mexicans the right to escape the misery in their own country and seek a better life in the United States – is not included. The bridge was opened without restriction, however, in September 1967, to permit Mexican refugees from Hurricane Beulah to seek the hospitality of the residents of Rio Grande City. (I remember Hurricane Beulah hitting the West Indies while I was on honeymoon in Antigua.) One can only guess at the number of Mexicans who never returned home, or who brought drugs with them among their meagre possessions.

The truism about the First World meeting the Third World at the Rio Grande – it is also the meeting-point of two countries and cultures, the one settled from northern Europe, the other from southern Europe – is obvious enough. Even in this relatively poor part of Texas, where Mexican names predominate, the contrasts are immediately apparent. Mexican houses are flat-roofed, generally made of adobe and coloured a faded pink or green. Texan houses have pitched roofs and are of wooden construction. Americans walk the streets with a purpose, going about their usually lawful occasions, whereas Mexicans loiter, not always giving an impression of lawful intent. As in other Third World countries, raggedly dressed children wander among grazing goats on rough ground on the outskirts of towns. In a US city, the grid system and the proliferation of street signs and signposts make it practically impossible to get lost. The reverse is true in Mexico, though once out of town it is a relief to find far fewer speed restriction signs and advertising hoardings at the roadside. It is the condition of the Mexican road surface which may limit your speed – and the occasional intervention by forces of the state. On Highway 2 north of Ciudad Miguel Aleman, four soldiers were diverting traffic on to the dusty, stony verge; whether this was done in order to inspect each vehicle for contraband or merely to assert their armed authority was not entirely clear.

In this border country, however, it is the similarities that are the more striking – which is hardly surprising when you consider that the Mexican Señor Perez on one side of the river and the Mexican-American Mr Perez on the other side not only share the same name but may quite possibly be related. Drug-smuggling across the border is more reliable, and much more secure, when it can be kept in the family. Mexican Texans, like all those of Latin stock, tend to live in tightly-knit, nuclear families; and when they are ill they go not to the doctor but to the local *curandero*, or some other lay healer. Look at any small border town in south Texas, and the names alone proclaim its Mexicanness. San Ygnacio, in Zapata County, has a 'Head Start Center' named after a Mexican president, Benito Juárez, and streets with the names of Mexican cities. Its elementary school is called Benavides, after a Sephardic Jewish family, Ben David, which emigrated to New Spain in the eighteenth century and played a significant part in Laredo's Mexican history.

Among the poor houses on either side of the Rio Grande, a modern, Spanish ranch-style house with a satellite dish on its roof sometimes sticks out – if not like a sore thumb, it proclaims itself no less obviously as a house built on drugs. 'Say Nope to Dope' the poster urged passers-by in Roma, but there was little chance that anyone would. Roma has a pretty eighteenth-century plaza, steamboats once came upriver as far as here, and part of the film *Viva Zapata!* was made in the town. Roma and Rio Grande City are the two border towns of Starr County where, it is said, smuggling is a way of life. Ever since a federal report estimated that thirty per cent of residents made money from the drugs trade, Starr County has had a bad press. It has also been described as one of the poorest counties of the nation, with around half its population on welfare benefits. But this is a black economy, and there is drugs money to be made. An officer from the Drug Enforcement Administration described what happens:

> There's a stash on the Mexican side that needs to cross. They'll need mules [carriers] to cross it, lookouts, skilled people to listen to radio scanners, people to drive trucks. So they find some twenty-year-old kids who're doing nothing Saturday night and who want to make a thousand dollars driving a truck from the river to town. They're all unemployed but after two weeks they're buying pickups and ostrich-skin cowboy boots with matching belts.

There is a long chain of payments (*mordidas*, little bites) to be made, many of them to public officials, who can then afford new houses. Mexico, you are told, has drug-enforcement agencies headed by people on the drug barons' payrolls. If the corruption doesn't go that deep in the federal USA, it certainly flourishes at the local level. At one time in the 1990s, of the thirteen counties in Texas which border the Rio Grande, seven had sheriffs who were under investigation, under indictment or in jail in connection with the drugs trade – not altogether surprising when a man is suddenly offered a tax-free sum of around ten times his annual salary. Smuggling has gone on across the river ever since it was formally recognised as the international border in 1848. Only the nature of the contraband has changed, bringing posses of law-enforcement officers to Texas and a lot of public money to combat the drugs traffic. But their efforts have been largely wasted: eighteen months after an operation in the 1970s led to the confiscation of quantities of marijuana and the conviction of a large number of people, the flow of drugs through Starr County was as great as before. The DEA will admit privately that their work has little long-term effect; the border will remain wide open. And small aeroplanes will continue to ferry drugs over the border with impunity. They are left alone, it is said, because they are not classified as enemy aircraft posing a threat to national security.

Upriver in Laredo, much of the contraband goes the other way. Whether on foot, by car, truck, train or plane, electronic goods, in particular, and arms pass down this Pan-American Highway which stretches from Canada to South America. Time was, in the 1970s, when Mexicans on a shopping trip to Laredo would return to Nuevo Laredo wearing three layers of newly purchased clothes and a couple of new suitcases filled with many more items. A *mordida* to the customs official, perhaps left lying on top of the clothes in the suitcase, would save any trouble. This practice has an honourable tradition: in the mid-nineteenth century a peripatetic US border commissioner, John Russell Bartlett, observed that 'the duty imposed by Mexico on many items of merchandise amounts to a prohibition. Yet owing to the laxity of customhouse officials the law has been evaded, and goods [have] regularly [been] admitted at a nominal rate.'

At one time there was so much smuggling by air that a Laredoan living near the airport said he could gauge the state of the city's economy by the number of DC3s he could hear taking off, loaded with electrical goods, for some remote landing strip in the Mexican desert beyond the

Sierra Madre. But things have changed somewhat since Mexico's entry into GATT (General Agreement on Tariffs and Trade) in 1986 and NAFTA in 1994. Import duties are still imposed, but only above a certain value; the volume of smuggled goods is not what it was. But the trade in weapons, to Central and South America, is increasing.

Laredo is the busiest border crossing of all – forty per cent of the land trade between the United States and Mexico crosses Laredo's three international road bridges and its nineteenth-century railway bridge. The latest bridge, opened in 2000 by the then US presidential candidate, George W. Bush, and the then Mexican president, Ernesto Zedillo, was built exclusively for trucks. Ten thousand trucks cross the border every day; for the last years of the 1990s, because the greatly increased trade generated a large supporting service industry, Laredo was declared to be the second fastest growing city in the USA. The average annual income for a Laredo employee – not including any bonuses from smuggling and corruption – was $23,000 at the end of the century, more than ten times the wage earned by a worker in the *maquiladoras* across the river.

The lorries heading south carry electronic equipment, lumber, wheat for all those tortillas (only six per cent of Mexico is arable land); while those bound for the United States may be loaded with cars containing caches of drugs in their fuel tanks – at risk of detection by X-ray or sniffer dogs. The perquisites of corruption, endemic in Mexico since time immemorial, are legion.

You cannot avoid hearing stories of illegal dealings between the two Laredos; one I found especially enjoyable – and no less enjoyable when I heard almost the same story but in relation to two other border towns: Brownsville and Matamoros. I don't know if it is apocryphal, but it certainly has the ring of truth. Young men are commonly hired to steal cars in Laredo and drive them over the border to Nuevo Laredo, where they find a ready market. A Texan woman, who had had her car stolen from outside her house, was in Nuevo Laredo one day with a friend when she spotted her car. They followed it in the friend's car until it drew up outside a house in an affluent residential suburb. A federal policeman stepped out and went indoors. The woman still had her car's spare key in her bag, so was able to retrieve her car and drive it back across the bridge to Laredo. The next day she had a telephone call from the policeman, who had noted her name and address from the car's registration documents. 'OK, you get your car back,' he said amiably, acknowledging that he had lost this particular game. 'But I need something back from you, please. I leave my pistol under the driver's seat.'

This, one might say, is but one aspect of the relationship between the two Laredos, more often called Los Dos Laredos. Unlike Brownsville, which was founded by Anglos at the end of the Mexican–American War, Laredo was first a Spanish town and then Mexican. Indeed for a long time it was the only Mexican town on the left bank of the Rio Grande. Then in 1840 the states of Tamaulipas, Nuevo Leon and Coahuila, which did not want to be governed from Mexico City, and Laredo, which did not want to be part of Texas, attempted a declaration of independence, establishing a Republic of the Rio Grande. But it lasted no more than nine months, and in 1848 all of Texas to the Rio Grande was formally ceded to the United States. Those Laredoans who did not wish to become Americans moved over the river to what had been the other half of their town.

Whereas Brownsville was originally dominated by Anglos, Laredo has always been overwhelmingly Hispanic. For almost a century, until 1978, the town was exclusively governed by the Spanish cacique system of dynastic power (the term is derived from the Indian word for chief). It began in fact with an Anglo rancher who married into the Escandon family, and ended with a grandson who was convicted of embezzling public funds. Nuevo Laredo remained under a cacique regime at the end of the twentieth century.

There is still today an association, even a community spirit, between Laredo and Nuevo Laredo that is closer than the relationship between any other of the 'twin' cities which face each other across the Rio Grande. *LareDOS* is the name of one local journal; another, the *Laredo Morning Times*, has a daily four-page section in Spanish, 'Tiempo de Laredo', which mostly carries news from Nuevo Laredo and elsewhere in Mexico. With a coupon from the *Laredo Morning Times*, you can get *El Diario de Nuevo Laredo* at a discount. The two towns share a baseball team – Tecolotes de los Dos Laredos – which plays in the Mexican League, sometimes on American soil. The mayors of the two Laredos join in annual celebrations of their shared heritage, embracing one another in the middle of one of the international bridges and singing the national anthems of both countries.

This practice is common to most border towns along the Rio Grande, but Laredo holds another popular celebration every year, in mid-February: it commemorates George Washington's birthday. It is unclear why Tex-Mex Laredo should wish to honour the Virginian first president of the United States, who governed at the end of the eighteenth century while Laredo was still part of the Spanish Empire. Presumably it has something to do with Washington being the liberating victor of the original revolution in the Americas. Mrs Washington is equally honoured in Laredo: each year the Society of Martha Washington holds a Colonial Pageant and Colonial Ball at which fourteen selected 'débutantes', suitably attired in colonial gowns supported by a variety of petticoats, crinolines and corsets, make a special appearance. Alongside them are an elegant-looking Hispanic couple, their not-so-white faces under powdered wigs, representing George and Martha Washington. The week's festivities continue with a Princess Pocahontas Pageant and Ball (she is also played, a bit more credibly, by a Mexican American), a Noche de Cabaret (which includes wine and cigar sampling), a cocktail party given by the Caballeros de la

Republica del Rio Grande and a huge fireworks display known as 'Thunder over Laredo'. In 1999, a luncheon was held for that year's Mr South Texas – a lady state senator, Judith Zaffirini, who despite protests was not permitted to call herself Mrs South Texas. And then comes the International Bridge Ceremony, held at eight o'clock in the morning after a sumptuous Mayor's Breakfast, if you can handle it at that time of day, offering 'authentic gourmet Mexican-style cuisine'. On the Juárez-Lincoln bridge, the Abrazo Children (the word means 'embrace') from Mexico and the USA, come together to do their bit, and the traditional words of welcome are spoken: 'Entre hermanos no hay fronteras.'

However, when Washington's birthday celebrations are over, some Texans of Hispanic descent in Laredo are less enthusiastic about the brotherhood of Mexicans for whom there are no frontiers. One commented:

> We came from there, but they're not us. They toss their garbage in the Rio Grande and want us to pay to clean it up. We may share a baseball team and a past, but we aren't one community. Who the hell wants to be part of Mexico?

That is the question. Few, having crossed the Rio Grande and tasted the American way of life and its earnings potential, want to go back to the Third World whence they came. One is often reminded of the saying: Pobre Mexico. Tan lejos de Dios y tan cerca de los Estados Unidos. Poor Mexico. So far from God and so close to the United States.

Close it may be, enabling Mexican Americans to cross the river frequently to visit family and friends, but they prefer to identify themselves with their adopted country. There was an incident at a United States v. Mexico soccer match in Los Angeles, when Mexican

⇜ Mexican Texas ⇜

Americans booed during the playing of the American national anthem and cheered for Mexico. But this was exceptional, and probably involved recent immigrants. The great majority of Mexican Americans, and certainly those living near the border, would not fail the Tebbit test of loyalty. Mexican–American border patrolmen do not flinch from arresting Mexicans trying to get to America; nor would American soldiers of Hispanic descent refuse to go to war in Central America. It is an interesting fact that Mexican Americans won more medals in the Second World War than any other sector of the American population. Many others, veterans of the Korean and Vietnam Wars, are likely to have crossed the tracks in their Texas border towns to live in an Anglo rather than a Chicano neighbourhood. A plaque outside Laredo proclaims, in Spanish as well as English, that US 83 is the Texas Vietnam Veterans' Memorial Highway; and a majority of those Texans killed in south-east Asia were Mexican Americans. (This statistic is no doubt due in part to the absence in Vietnam of those of the Anglo middle class who, like the future President Clinton, were able to avoid military service.) This conspicuous record of Mexican-American loyalty to the United States is impressive indeed, but it can lead to vexed questions about patriotism in Mexican–American history. When the first American immigrants arrived in Texas in the 1820s, it was part of the Mexican state of Coahuila. Not unreasonably, they were required, and agreed, to become Mexican citizens, speak Spanish and abide by Mexican law. But they are not condemned for not having done so. When those first Texans revolted against the country which let them in, were they patriots or traitors? Perhaps one would be better advised to Remember the Alamo and not ask that question.

Mexico may have been the loser to the United States throughout its history, but it can produce a larger flag. Seemingly intent on demonstrating it can do something bigger, if not better, than its otherwise superior neighbour, the town of Nuevo Laredo flies a Mexican flag on its riverbank which is almost the size of an American football pitch. Laredo Texans may patronisingly see it as a bit of a joke, but they certainly cannot avoid seeing it. Visitors to Nuevo Laredo, as to other Mexican border towns, are greeted at the customs post by a satirical-sounding sign: 'Las armas son illegales en Mexico.' It is an awful thought that if weapons were legal the statistics for armed crime in Mexico would be even worse than they are already. Superficially, Nuevo Laredo is like other border towns, with its central Plaza Juárez, market stalls, sandstone and brick buildings, *maquiladoras* on the outskirts, dust and smells and seediness. New Laredo undoubtedly looks older than Old Laredo, and more familiar with the seamy side of life. It has what Texans will tell you is the most famous Boys' Town along the border. Other towns have their red-light areas (*zonas rojas* or *zonas de tolerancia*), but Nuevo Laredo's is supposedly *numero uno*.

A couple of miles from the international bridge, past the rail depot and just off the main road to Monterrey, my taxi turned through an entrance guarded by a police officer and into a large, unpaved compound, its stony surface pitted with holes. The *zona* must have been almost a hectare in size: ahead was the Casino El Papagayo and the Club Miramar; around the yard were rows of doors which had not been painted in a long while. It was midday, and it all looked depressingly sordid and run-down. There was no darkness or neon lighting to create an illusion; but the place was open for business. The taxi-driver stopped outside the Tanayko club – 'the Japanese are the best,' he advised. Next door a Donkey's Show was advertised. He went on to tell me that the Miramar was the place for *las chicos*, a neat double-gender way of describing transvestite prostitutes, who apparently appeal to, or provide amusement for some Texan truck drivers, salesmen and college boys.

At this time of day, *las chicos* were probably eating refried beans and shaving their legs; it was not an appealing thought. Many of the prostitutes would have come to Boys' Town by way of the *maquiladoras*, where they tired of stitching sweatshirts all day for less than $10. Back in the centre of Nuevo Laredo, everything quickly improved over a margarita at the El Dorado, a seventy-year-old bar and restaurant (once called the Cadillac) with the atmosphere of a gentleman's London club. There are bucks' heads on the walls, green 'leather' armchairs, rotating ceiling fans and a dark-wooden bar some forty feet long. An elderly pianist was playing 'Love is a many splendour'd thing' in the corner. On an extensive list of dozens of named cocktails, I noted Grasshopper, Deep Throat and Colorado Bulldog; a dish of *cabrito asado* (roast kid) and a bottle of Mexican red wine soon banished unpleasant thoughts of *las chicos* and the stomach-upsetting food more usually associated with Mexico.

Roast kid is a speciality of northern Mexican cooking, and about the only one I really enjoyed. My problem with Tex/Mex and Cal/Mex border food is not that it is too spicy – I enjoy Indian and oriental cooking – but that it is too heavy. The description, for instance, of *enchiladas* which I came across in an English-language book on Mexican cuisine – 'meat or cheese wrapped in tortillas and smothered in red or green salsa, cream and melted cheese' – surely makes the point clearly enough. Avoiding melted cheese in Mexican cooking can be tricky. *Fajitas* – a rather tasty Chinese-style dish of chicken or beef, cooked with sliced onions and peppers – are cheeseless; but when I once asked for them in a restaurant in Ciudad Juárez, I was informed that:'We only serve authentic Mexican food; *fajitas* are Tex-Mex.' Farther south, Mexicans enthuse over their national sauce, *mole*, made with chiles and chocolate, and the Pueblan speciality *chile en nogada*. This, according to the same cookbook, is ' a green *chile poblano* stuffed with a stew of beef and fruits, topped with a walnut sauce and adorned with pomegranate seeds'. One hopes it isn't adorned with anything else, such as melted cheese or *frijoles refritos*, the popular dish of mashed and fried beans. (President Fox has said that he eats three plates of beans a day to give him the energy to run the country.)

❧ Mexican Texas ❦

Graham Greene was very rude about Mexican food. Writing in *The Lawless Roads* about a lunch in Nuevo Laredo, he found it

> ...awful: like the food you eat in a dream, tasteless in a positive way, so that the very absence of taste is repellent. All Mexican food is like that: if it isn't hot with sauces, it's nothing at all ... After a while your palate loses all discrimination; hunger conquers; you begin in a dim way even to look forward to your meal. I suppose if you live long enough in Mexico you begin to write like Miss Frances Toor* – 'Mexican cooking appeals to the eye as well as to the palate.' (It is all a hideous red and yellow, green and brown, like art needlework and the sort of cushions popular among decayed gentlewomen in Cotswold teashops.)

My advice to anyone with tastes similar to mine is to stick to tortillas (made from wheat in the north and corn, i.e. maize, elsewhere in the country), with salsa or a salad of tomatoes, onions and coriander; and to eat grilled white fish and shellfish wherever possible and without *mole*. There is a chain of restaurants serving delicious fish called Los Arcos, and one can be found in most of the major cities. The best-known chain is Sanborn's, excellent for breakfasts without cheese and chile sauces. In Mexico City, Sanborn's is housed in the Casa de los Azulejos, where the early-twentieth-century revolutionary leaders used to plot with and against one another.

A lot of raw sewage and chemicals get pumped into the Rio Grande; some of the pollution comes from the *maquiladoras*, and virtually all of it comes from Mexico. Doctors advise against eating fish caught any-

*An American author who published books on Mexico in the 1930s and 1940s.

where in the river. An acquaintance told me he had seen a chicken go down to the river to drink, take a few sips, lift its head and fall dead. I looked down on this unclean water from the middle of the Juárez-Lincoln bridge. Next to a sign announcing a $200 fine for dropping rubbish into the river, a Mexican girl was idly eating a grapefruit and letting the peel fall on to half-submerged tyres and weed-covered wooden planks. How could she be fined five weeks' wages when the foreign company in Nuevo Laredo which employed her might suffer no penalty for an offence a thousand times more serious? The *maquiladora* would answer that the bad old days of dumping toxic waste in the river are over, that since NAFTA each country is responsible for enforcing its own environmental standards, that assembly plants have been shut down by the Mexican authorities for pollution offences. But the water still looks horribly polluted.

A little way downstream, I could see four Mexicans, their clothes on their heads, wading across the river – *mojados* who hoped that by keeping their clothes dry they would fool the border guards into thinking they had crossed by the bridge. They hid in tall rushes on the Texas bank, only a few yards from a waiting Border Patrol vehicle, which could not immediately see them. Next to me on the bridge, someone was signalling to the concealed would-be immigrants. A green-uniformed Mexican-American officer, who had presumably been watching the signals, then got out of the vehicle and peered casually into the rushes from the top of the bank. But he wasn't going to investigate any more closely – it was mid-afternoon on a very hot day – and he soon returned to the air-conditioned comfort of his Cherokee.

No one attempted to climb up the bank, and ten minutes later three of the prospective immigrants waded and swam back to the Mexican shore. One man returned to the rushes on the Laredo side, then paddled back (or was it someone else?) to Mexico and sat down in some thorn bushes. By now I was getting confused. A flock of grackles (noisy relatives of the mocking bird) skittered across the water from the Mexican bank into the Texas rushes, as if drawing attention to the one (or was it more?) Mexican who was still hidden there. But the Border Patrol decided there was nothing to stay for and drove off to search farther downstream. It amazed me that Mexicans would think they could get into the USA undetected in daylight and so close to an international bridge. But I was told later by a shopkeeper of one woman who forded the Rio Grande from Nuevo Laredo and was apprehended three times in one day. He compared it to bass fishing: 'You go after them, catch them after a bit of a struggle, toss them back, and catch them again the next day.' The border was not really a deterrent; more of a challenge – a match or contest with an outside chance of winning. When I went through the US Customs post into Laredo, I passed a notice, 'Piso Mojado', and wondered momentarily at the use of this politically incorrect term in print. Then I realised that I was only being warned that the floor in the customs building was wet – though not from dripping clothes out of the river.

That night a retired Anglo border guard told me it used to bother him sometimes that the illegal immigrants he was detaining and sending back to Mexico were descended from people who lived here first, before Texas became a part of the United States. What bothered him even more were the coyotes, who undertake to deliver aliens into the USA for an exorbitant fee that they can ill afford. Many are Central Americans (from Nicaragua and Guatemala) who spend weeks travelling through Mexico, getting ripped off and raped along the way, only to have the last of their savings taken from them by the coyotes who get them across the Rio Grande. There is, of course, no guarantee that they will not then be caught. When I left Laredo the following morning, heading north, there was a Border Patrol helicopter flying low a few hundred yards from the road, hoping to spot any Mexicans who had successfully forded the river during the night. Now and again it turned, hovered and dipped over the mesquite scrub, like a hawk preparing to dive on its prey.

If you wonder at the desperation of Mexicans ready to hand over their savings in order to escape from their country, living conditions in the border-town *colonias* offer a compelling enough reason. There is no running water or sewerage in these miserable shanties which, if they have walls, have only holes for windows half-boarded-up against the weather. You assume that these *casas de carton* must have been abandoned, until you see a washing-line with clothes hanging on it. In most large border towns the *colonias* are some way from the Rio Grande, but in Piedras Negras I saw hovels on the riverbank, roofed with loose pieces of corrugated tin and by almost any standard uninhabitable, which stood no more than two hundred yards from the American Dream. And what happens if the short crossing is safely made from Mexico to the United States, avoiding the law-enforcement officers of the Immigration and Naturalization Service? The chances are that the new immigrant family will be delivered by the overpaid coyote into a Texas *colonia* also lacking the services of water and sanitation. But the hygiene must be a bit better. Children on the right bank of the river are four times more likely to die before their first birthday than are their American neighbours on the left.

The Indians seem to do a lot better than the Mexicans. As a migrant, tribal people, they have always moved freely between Mexico and the United States, and it is the policy of the US Border Patrol not to bother them. Kickapoo Indians, whose ancestral home is at Nacimiento, Coahuila, south of Piedras Negras, used to spend much of the year living under the international bridge between Piedras Negras and Eagle Pass. During the summer months, however, they would become migrant workers, picking cotton in Texas, lifting sugar beet in Utah and Idaho, harvesting cherries in the Great Lakes states. Then, in the 1970s, the Department of Housing and Urban Development agreed to underwrite some land and a village for the Kickapoo outside Eagle Pass. They established a reservation, and built themselves houses, thatched- or tin-roofed, eight miles away, appropriately off the El Indio road. And they started the Lucky Eagle Casino, which is operated entirely for the benefit of the Kickapoo, who don't need to travel across America doing seasonal labour any more. Why do Indians run casinos in Texas and other states when nobody else does? Basically because, while state law may not permit gaming, Indians are subject only to federal law, which does. In El Paso, Tigua Indians run the Speaking Rock Casino, next to their Cultural Center. Here tourists pay to watch Tigua tribal dances and listen to their chants, not knowing that the Indians are mostly ignorant of these rituals and have had to be taught them by an anthropologist from New Mexico.

Piedras Negras, named after the black rocks of this coal-mining district, is one of the pleasanter Mexican border towns. The international bridge leads at once to an open plaza, grassed in the middle, with palm trees, wrought-iron bandstands and a fine church on the far side. It is certainly a more attractive place than its Texan twin, Eagle Pass, which has a romantic name but little else to recommend it. The name (which sounds even better in its Mexican version: El Paso del Aguila) suggests circling birds of prey, crags, high tops, a river winding through a deep gorge. But there is no hilly country here, merely a few bluffs, and not an eagle to be seen above this dismal little town, which has only a tenth of the population of Piedras Negras. In recent years, this has become a much-used crossing for illegal drugs, especially marijuana smuggled by backpackers. South of Eagle Pass, many families have given up their properties along the river because they felt threatened by the violence inevitably associated with drugs trafficking. The worry now is that the land put up for sale is being acquired by drug-smugglers.

❧ Mexican Texas ❧

Eagle Pass's appeal lies all in the past. At the time of the Civil War, it was the one town in Texas to reject the Confederacy, and by an overwhelming majority. Union supporters found it safer, though, to spend the war on the other side of the river, in Piedras Negras, while the Confederate General Joseph O. Shelby occupied the Texan frontier post of Fort Duncan. During the temporary Union occupation of Brownsville, he arranged the transport of cotton across the river, with appropriate payments to Mexican customs officers, and thence by road to Matamoros and Bagdad. Returning to Eagle Pass in 1865, the Unionists jeered Shelby and his brigade as they made their way south to join the Habsburg Mexican Emperor Maximilian – and suffer another defeat when the hapless Austrian was executed a couple of years later. The demise of Maximilian was celebrated with a ball in Piedras Negras, to which 'all the best people' in Eagle Pass were invited.

In the second half of the nineteenth century, Eagle Pass, part of the Texas 'Badlands', would have been filled with cattle rustlers, bandits and Indians. A border freebooter called Callahan once crossed the river from Eagle Pass with a band of followers to recover some negro slaves who had escaped from him into Mexico. Having encountered and defeated a superior force of Mexican soldiers, he occupied and looted Piedras Negras for several days before being persuaded to return by the commander at Fort Duncan. Eagle Pass was also on the main trade routes for the wagon-trains carrying cotton from San Antonio to Mexico City – which was how a remarkable Scots traveller and Renaissance man, with his wife, came to pass through this frontier town in 1880.

Robert Cunninghame Graham belonged to a landed family, with property in Perthshire and on the Isle of Bute; after Harrow and a private school in Brussels he took himself off to South America, where he rode and coped horses for a few years. Then in 1878 he met and married Gabriela de la Balmondière, said to be of French-Chilean blood. In fact she was born Caroline Horsfall in Yorkshire, and changed her name when, having run away from home, she embarked on a career on the stage in Paris, where she met Cunninghame Graham. The following year they sailed for Texas, via New Orleans, and stayed briefly in Brownsville (which did not appeal to them) and Corpus Christi, before moving up to San Antonio, which Graham found more tolerable. But he would rather have been back in Argentina. To his mother he wrote disparagingly of Texas and the Texans:

> The country is very ugly all covered with dense low scrub and not such a thing as an open pampa. The people of all the people I ever came across are revolting and mean to a degree. The Mexicans are the only redeeming feature and they are not strictly speaking agreeable as they are chiefly thieves and murderers exiled from Mexico.

In San Antonio, from the comfort of the Menger Hotel, with its gold-plated spittoons, the Grahams enjoyed listening to the hay-dealers and fruit-sellers shouting in Spanish in the square outside. Having bought a consignment of cotton, they set off with their mule train at the beginning of 1880, taking seven weeks to reach Mexico City. Each night the wagons were formed into a square, secured with ropes against the constant danger of marauding bandits and Apaches. Beans, bacon and rough bread were cooked over a camp-fire in the middle, and they slept either round the fire or on bales of cotton in the wagons. After a week of riding across the flat scrubland to Eagle Pass, they crossed the river to Piedras Negras, described by Gabriela Graham as 'a den of contrabandists, thieving customhouse officers and mongrel Americans, kept in order by a beggarly, bare-footed crew of soldiers, of which seven hundred, cavalry and infantry, are always in the barracks'.

She had nothing good to say about Eagle Pass and its inhabitants – 'the wooden shanty of the American, in all its appalling ugliness, his tinned meats and his universal shoddy' – preferring the 'brown and picturesque' Mexicans and their Hispano-Mauresque architecture. 'They like lounging about in their plazas, dressed in wide white drawers, a sarape thrown carelessly over the shoulder, glowering suspiciously at the stranger, and gloomily calculating what amount of profit might possibly accrue from a quick stab of the knife dexterously driven home into that stranger's shoulder.' When bargaining for goods, Mrs Graham's experience was that the Mexican 'contents himself by demanding two-thirds more than the price he means to take eventually'. Her observations generally hold good today, though one may take issue with her comment that, to her eye, the countryside outside Piedras Negras resembled parts of Wales.

As they proceeded south across the grey-green, scrubby plains, the Grahams saw herds of deer and antelope, wild turkeys and boar and later, in the mountains, they had to beware of bears and wolves as well as *bandidos*, one of whom, a member of their party, planned to rob and kill them. When they at last reached Mexico City – by way of Saltillo and San Luis Potosí – they booked into a French hotel, 'luxuriously supping on côtelettes à la milanaise and a bottle of burgundy'. But the cotton was sold at a loss.

In spite of his prolific literary output, Cunninghame Graham did not record his impressions of Mexico City. But he published a sketch, 'A Hegira', which gives an account of their return to Texas. Eagle Pass does not get a mention; had he been there four years later he would surely have remarked on the town's new courthouse, then being built, which remains today the one building of which Eagle Pass can be proud. Flanked by palm trees, it has crenellations beneath a handsome clock tower, tall arched windows and white stucco walls. (Another Victorian traveller, Mrs Alec Tweedie, may have seen it when she crossed the border by train at Eagle Pass to begin her travels in Mexico, which would yield three books published in the early years of the twentieth century. Piedras Negras was then called Ciudad Porfirio Díaz, after the country's dictator president, and Mrs Tweedie's hero.)*

Graham devotes part of his sketch to a bitterly sarcastic denunciation of the treatment meted out to the Indians. Throughout his life he was vigorously opposed to racial bigotry and imperialism. After becoming Liberal MP for North Lanarkshire in 1886, he was a well-known champion of the working classes, and of the Irish. He was jailed for his part in the Free Speech Riots in Trafalgar Square, demonstrating on behalf of an Irish MP, and he was the only English MP to attend Parnell's funeral. Though he lost his parliamentary seat in 1892, Graham co-founded the Scottish Labour Party (with Keir Hardie) and in later life was the Scottish National Party's first president. But he also continued to spend much of his time travelling – in Spain and Morocco as well as Latin America – and writing. For a number of years he was friendly with Joseph Conrad, who dedicated one of his sea stories, *Typhoon*, to him. He was sent to South America to buy horses during the First World War and at the end of his life, at the age of eighty-three, he went back to his favourite country, Argentina, where he died in 1936.

Cunninghame Graham was painted more than once by his friend Sir John Lavery. The best-known portrait is full length and, most appropriately, in the style of Velazquez; it hangs in the Glasgow Art Gallery. The bearded subject stands confidently, if not arrogantly, in a long black coat, with cane and gloves and a rather bohemian scarlet neckerchief, loosely tied. George Bernard Shaw, who used Graham as his model for Captain Brassbound, wrote of him: 'He is, I understand, a Spanish *hidalgo*, hence the superbity of his portrait by Lavery (Velazquez being no longer available).' Lavery also painted him on his black horse, Pampa; this picture belongs to the Museo de Bellas Artes in Buenos Aires but hangs in the presidential palace.

---

* *see pages 27-28.*

Mexican Texas

During his stay in south-west Texas, Graham had spent some time breaking mustangs, guiding buffalo hunters and driving cattle. With a Mexican Greek he formed a ranching partnership close to the border, commenting in a letter: 'I am getting more reconciled to Texas [though] Mexico is a much nicer country.' He also met Buffalo Bill (Colonel William Cody) who was then starting the Wild West Show which he would later bring to Europe. It was during a visit to London that one of his troupe, a Sioux chief known as Long Wolf, died and was buried in the Brompton cemetery. Graham recalled this in an article first published in 1921: he knew nothing of Long Wolf's life, but wondered if he might have fought at Little Bighorn, in what was General Custer's last stand. Long Wolf had died in 1892; a wolf was sculptured on the cross above his grave and, according to Graham, artificial pansies were placed on the ground in two glass cases. This strange memorial, recording the death of an Indian chief and giving only his assumed tribal name, was still to be found in the Brompton cemetery more than a hundred years later. But then someone thought to trace Long Wolf's living descendants, and at the end of the century his remains were exhumed, in the presence of a large gathering of his Indian relatives chanting round the grave. After a service in a nearby church, the old chief, in a coffin draped with the American flag, was repatriated to his homeland in South Dakota. Graham would have been disappointed: he liked to imagine that at night the carved wolf would come to life, its melancholy howl resounding all over west London.

Big Bend

Chapter Four

Slow Train to Misery Pass

DEL RIO is two or three miles from the river, but it has plenty of water thanks to underground springs, which explain the town's familiar name, La Reina del Rio Grande. Natural irrigation makes for good ranching country (Angora goats are raised here for their mohair) and the viability of Texas's oldest and only surviving commercial vineyard. North of Del Rio there is the seventy thousand-acre Lake Amistad (Friendship), a reservoir formed by the building of the Amistad dam as a joint US–Mexican project in the 1960s. Presidents Nixon and Díaz Ordaz were the first two leaders to stage a meeting, as a token of their friendship, on the newly completed road over the dam. Since then the mayors of Del Rio and its neighbouring town in Coahuila, Ciudad Acuña, have met annually on top of the dam for an *abrazo*, or goodwill embrace. At other times of the year they meet, rather more comfortably, in each other's offices or town halls.

At this ceremony they are each attended by a colour guard, a school band and a young female representative of their town. Miss Del Rio, who is a classmate of Señorita Ciudad Acuña, hands her a stick of chewing gum. Below them, water-skiers cross repeatedly from one country to the other. Even military officers embrace at the border point, under the gaze of their two national eagles, sculpted in bronze. Closer inspection reveals that while the Mexican eagle, perched on a prickly pear cactus, holds the traditional writhing serpent in its mouth, its American counterpart, with an olive branch in one talon, does not have the usual cluster of arrows in the other. On a day when the mayor of Del Rio is mouthing platitudes about the two countries being joined, not divided, by the river, this may be considered a tactful and sensitive modification. But no one supposes that the arrows will be put away for long.

Del Rio is also on the railway line, which is how I came to pass through it on the train from Houston to El Paso. Amtrak, which runs the passenger rail service in the United States, has to operate under the disadvantage that the rail track belongs to the freight companies who, understandably enough, put their own interests first. Amtrak may not have advance warning of track repairs and consequent delays to their services. Our train, having arrived before dawn in San Antonio, had to wait for three hours to link up with another train coming from Chicago, which had been badly delayed. Having glimpsed Lake Amistad beyond Del Rio, we then stopped out in the country for the best part of an hour – not due to work on the line or an approaching freight train on a stretch of single track, but because, as an attendant put it, an old lady had been 'taken real bad, and passed away in a diabetic coma'. Fortunately there was a doctor on board to sign the death certificate, but then we had to wait for a local sheriff to arrive and remove the body.

Sitting in the observation car at the time, I fell in with a black grandmother from California, who boasted of having twenty-five grandchildren. Perhaps to escape from them for a while, she had been travelling by train for the past three weeks, as far as Chicago, Washington DC and New Orleans. 'After all the rippin' and runnin' back home, the train gives you the chance to lay back and learn a bit about this country of ours,' she said. You need to have time to spare to travel by train in the United States. A little later we stopped again because a 'malfunction' had been detected and an unfortunate railman had to walk along the track, checking every coupling, in a temperature of 100°F. Given the vast network of internal airlines, the standard of all main highways and the price of petrol, it is hardly surprising that the railways (for long-distance journeys at least) come a poor third. At Houston, the fourth largest city in the United States, the station building consists of nothing more than a seedy waiting-room, a few old wooden benches and a ticket office which was closed before the night train arrived at 11 p.m.

But you do get to meet some interesting people on the train. I told my new acquaintance that when I had taken the train a few years ago, from Washington to New Orleans, I had shared a table in the dining-car with a blind man. I remember he asked me to pour some milk on his hominy grits and describe the country we were passing through. On my return journey I met a woman – a photographer who did some work for *National Geographic* magazine – who had travelled by train from her home near Tucson, Arizona. She had lived in the desert for five years, had seldom seen a newspaper during that time and was unaware who was president of her country. She was going to Maine to take pictures of the sandhill crane.

During another unscheduled stop in the middle of nowhere, while I was staring idly at an unrelieved landscape of mesquite scrub and distant hills, a roadrunner, with a worm wriggling in its beak, hopped on to a dead branch outside the window. A woman next to me passed on the information that it was somewhere along this stretch of line that a group of wetbacks had recently died from suffocation, trapped in locked boxcars. Complaining that the train must now be more than four hours late, she said she was going to El Paso to see her son who was a Border Patrol guard.

By now we were close to Langtry, a Wild West outpost of the late nineteenth century where Judge Roy Bean famously declared himself to be the 'law west of the Pecos'. When the Southern Pacific Railway was built, Bean was an itinerant who sold whiskey to the workforce and somehow talked himself into the job of Langtry's first justice of the peace. It is said that he named the town after his favourite actress, Lillie

Langtry. This may or may not be true, but the judge did run a saloon which he called the Jersey Lily (it doubled as bar and courtroom). And in 1896 he turned boxing promoter when a championship fight between Bob Fitzsimmons and Peter Maher, due to take place in El Paso, was cancelled by Texas officials at the last minute. Judge Bean saw his opportunity and invited the contestants to Langtry instead. He cleverly avoided any interference from the Texas authorities by erecting a boxing ring on a strip of land along the Mexican bank of the Rio Grande and constructing a pontoon bridge to bring the crowds across. The fight didn't last beyond the first round – Fitzsimmons knocked out his Irish opponent – but the spectators spent the rest of the night happily filling Judge Bean's coffers in his Jersey Lily saloon. Eight years later, Lillie Langtry apparently passed through the town on a private train, but by then the judge was dead and buried in Del Rio.

It was near Langtry that John Grady forded the river into Mexico, in the first of Cormac McCarthy's acclaimed Border Trilogy of novels, *All the Pretty Horses*. Having ridden down the Pecos River valley from Pandale, he made his way through the Serranias de Burro and south as far as Saltillo, where he had a spell in jail before returning to Texas. McCarthy, who lives in El Paso, has enjoyed great critical and popular success with his Border Trilogy. His writing has been compared to William Faulkner's. It is barren, rugged and often beautiful, like the country of south-west Texas and northern Mexico which he writes about. Saul Bellow has written of McCarthy's 'almost overpowering use of language... life-giving and death-dealing sentences'. However, the dialogue, written without quotation marks and some of it in Spanish, can, in my opinion, become irritating at times.

The first novel is set in the late 1940s. John Grady, a teenager from an old ranching family and his two young companions are set on pursuing the life of the Old West. One of them is killed in Mexico and the other two, hardened by their experiences, soon grow older than their years.

⇥ SLOW TRAIN TO MISERY PASS ⇤

As they ride towards the border at the beginning of their adventures, Grady consults a map that shows

> roads and rivers and towns on the American side of the map as far south as the Rio Grande and beyond that all was white.
> It don't show nothin down there, does it? said Rawlins.
> No.
> You reckon it aint never been mapped?
> There's maps. That just aint one of em. I got one in my saddlebag.
> Rawlins came back with the map and sat on the ground and traced their route with his finger. He looked up.
> What? said John Grady.
> There aint shit down there.

Nor is there much habitation south of the New Mexico/Arizona border, where McCarthy's second novel, *The Crossing*, is set, a decade before the first one. Another young cowboy, Billy Parham, is unable to resist the lure of Mexico, the first time riding into the mountains with a wolf in tow. 'You just got a wild hair up your ass and there wouldnt nothin else do but for you to go off to Mexico,' the local sheriff tells him when he returns home. He learns that his parents have been killed, and he heads south again, this time with his brother, Boyd, who gets shot and dies. On his third trip he rides over the Chihuahua desert in search of Boyd's remains. In the last book of the trilogy, *Cities of the Plain*, Grady and Parham are together, working on a ranch near Orogrande, New Mexico. Much of the action, and the final tragedy, take place just over the border in Ciudad Juárez.

The railway, and the main road (Highway 90), leave the river after Langtry. Our train seemed to leave its troubles behind as we proceeded at reasonable speed and without any more unscheduled stops. But I couldn't help comparing Amtrak's performance with the Japanese bullet trains on which I had travelled the previous year. The Texas landscape, however, was more attractive to my eye than the urbanised plains south of Tokyo. The few towns that we passed owe their existence to the railway, built in the 1880s. Today they remain little more than settlements sitting at the junctions of the only roads to go through this desolate country. It was a surprise to see an antique shop and an art gallery in Marathon and, in Alpine (named because of its situation, at 4,500 feet), a red-brick university built in neo-classical style. It would be more imposing and impressive were there not a large McDonald's sign in front, and rows of little red-brick Monopoly houses which are used as married students' quarters. After the miles of plains and scrub and rocky crags, however, it was something of a relief to come upon what passes for civilisation in these parts.

At the station I saw a notice advertising a restaurant which offered 'Texas Cowboy Cuisine'. It was called Reata, which stirred a distant memory. My recollection became sharper when we stopped at the next town, Marfa, and a fellow passenger remarked that *Giant* had been filmed in these parts. The principal actors had stayed at the El Paisano Hotel in Marfa, while filming on location nearby, and there was a mural of James Dean on a horse in the Reata restaurant in Alpine. Now it was all coming back: Rock Hudson, Elizabeth Taylor and James Dean (it was one of only three feature films in which he appeared). *Giant* won an Oscar for best director (George Stevens) in 1956. Reata was the vast Texas property owned by a cattle baron, Jordan Benedict (Rock Hudson), on which the sullen farmhand, Jett Rink (James Dean), strikes oil and becomes fabulously rich. The house is gloriously absurd: a turn-of-the-century mansion standing in a vast and dusty plain framed by distant mountains. Its ruins, I was told, could still be seen a few miles from Marfa.

The story of the film, which I watched once again on videotape, spans a quarter of a century, ending in the 1960s. Benedict's son, who wants to become a doctor rather than take on the family ranch, marries a Mexican, Juana, whom Jordan Benedict stands up for, if only to avoid public humiliation for the family. In a memorable scene towards the end, Rock Hudson gets involved in a fight with the owner of a roadside diner who refuses to serve his daughter-in-law. The film ends with Elizabeth Taylor saying how proud she was of her husband when he ended up on the floor of the diner, with his head in a pile of dirty plates, and Rock Hudson coming to terms with the fact that his grandson Jordan Benedict IV 'looks like a little wetback'. In terms of race relations, *Giant* was some way ahead of its time.

South of Marfa, the road leads over mountains inhabited by pronghorn antelope and through the old silver-mining town of Shafter, to the river and border bridge at Presidio, said to be the hottest place in the United States. From Alpine and from Marathon the roads go into the Big Bend National Park, where the Rio Grande, having flowed southeast all the way from El Paso, now turns sharply northward as it passes from Chihuahua into Coahuila on the Mexican side. Here the river winds between vertical limestone canyon walls, at times so close together that boatmen claim to have touched the two countries simultaneously with their oars. In places the sun penetrates to the river for only a brief period around midday, while the tops of the cliffs turn a brilliant orange towards sundown. Below, the river is often muddy and little islands of silt reveal themselves when the water level falls. Not much may appear to live or grow among the rocks, gravel and volcanic debris, but naturalists will produce long lists of wildlife and plants to be found in this area. Sandpipers, blue quail and a curiously named ring-plover called killdeer are to be seen along the riverbank, and mountain lion are likely to be out hunting at night. In the Boquillas Canyon wild horses have made tracks through the overgrown sandbanks on both sides of the river. The vegetation hereabouts consists mainly of prickly pear, agave and the tall stalks of ocotillo, not to mention the ubiquitous creosote bush, which smells of tar. High above the river, where aspens grow at above seven thousand feet, the rocky pinnacles can be seen falling away to foothills which slope towards the arid wastes of the Mexican desert.

This stretch of the Rio Grande, some three hundred and fifty miles through the Big Bend, was considered impassable until 1899, when an officer of the US Geological Survey, Robert Hill, undertook the trip with five companions and three specially built boats. They had to contend with rapids, a notorious Mexican bandit known as 'Old White Lip' and with rockfalls from the awesome, vertical chocolate-coloured sides of the canyons which threatened to enclose them. Their greatest fear was that if the boats were wrecked, or if rising waters made further progress impossible, there was no other way out. In one particularly dark and twisting canyon, with only a narrow ribbon of sky above them, Hill recorded gloomily: 'For its entire length there is no place where this cliff can be climbed by man.' When the expedition finally reached Langtry, the six men had been rowing ten hours a day for more than a month.

In the Boquillas Canyon, named for the 'little mouths' of light between the towering walls, there is what is known as an 'unofficial border crossing', between Rio Grande Village on the Texas side and Boquillas del Carmen in Coahuila. A boat called *La Enchilada* ferries visitors and residents across during the day, and for those entering Mexico mules can be hired for the one-mile trip into town; but of the US Border Patrol and the Mexican customs there is no sign. Nor will any electricity, telephone or public transport be found in Boquillas del Carmen. If any medical help, or anything that comes from a refrigerator, is required, it is available a few minutes away across the Rio Grande. The best thing to do here is admire the jagged peaks of the Sierra del Carmen – and the vision of President Franklin Roosevelt who said in 1944 that the Big Bend National Park 'will not be complete until the entire park area in this region on both sides of the Rio Grande forms one great international park'. Rotarians from both countries worked for years to establish such a 'peace park', covering more than two million acres, and it was agreed in principle in 1997 by the US and Mexican Secretaries of the Interior, marking an important step in environmental cooperation between the two countries.

The flora and fauna of the region may be protected, but such a sparsely settled border area is, of course, always good for smuggling – and not only of people and drugs. Candelilla is a pencil-thin cactus which grows in the deserts of Chihuahua and Coahuila and, after boiling and processing, produces a wax which puts the crucial chew into chewing gum. For decades Mexicans have carried candelilla across the river, using mules, though the industry has declined in recent years. Local names – Contrabando Creek, Las Vegas de los Ladrones (The Plains of the Thieves) – bear witness to what goes, or used to go, on.

Legitimate industries in this border area have in the past concentrated on mining: cinnabar, for mercury, used to be mined at Study Butte (Stoody Beaut) near Lajitas, which still looks like a town of the Old West and today offers catfish from the Rio Grande at the Badlands Hotel. But the fluorspar mines, jointly owned by DuPont and sundry Mexican investors, have kept going. They are situated just south of the border, and the powdered raw material, which is a prime ingredient of fluorocarbon, is put on freight trains at Marathon. Some of the Mexican workforce inevitably cross the river (with shoes and clothing provided by the mining company) and find work in Texas instead.

The small towns and villages along the east and west banks of the Rio Grande are in many ways indistinguishable. Whether Texan or Mexican, they have Spanish-speaking populations, most of them living in one-storey adobe houses. The tiny Texan border town of Redford, whose residents call it El Polvo (Dust), receives and delivers letters addressed to the inhabitants of *pueblos* on the other side of the river. This possibly illegal arrangement makes perfect sense, because the nearest Mexican sorting office is at least two hours' drive away in Ojinaga, and the vast majority of mail for these border *pueblos* comes from addresses in Texas. One can understand here why the Texan–Mexican border is sometimes referred to as a 'third nation'. You don't find such informal cooperation between Alta and Baja California. But it would be a mistake to imagine that the Border Patrol takes a more relaxed attitude to *indocumentados* along this remote stretch of the border. And the toughest, most aggressive Border Patrol officers, I was told, are Hispanic. Law enforcement here is best described as arbitrary, and there is not much prospect of redress for what may politely be called an 'excess of zeal' by the authorities. In 1997 a young goatherd, Ezequiel Hernandez, was going about his business outside Redford when he was shot dead by a US marine engaged in drugs surveillance, on detachment with the Border Patrol. The incident caused such a furore that it went as far as a grand jury, but only a jury stacked with federal employees who were never likely to side with a poor Hispanic against a law-enforcement officer. An illegal alien (which Hernandez wasn't) is more likely to get away once he has crossed the railway line and Highway 90, heading probably for Fort Stockton and then on to Midland Odessa.

South of Presidio, where the road from Marfa crosses the border and at the junction of the Rio Grande and the Rio Conchos, Ojinaga commemorates the intrepid sixteenth-century explorer Alvar Núñez Cabeza de Vaca as a healer who bridged the gap between Spanish and Indian culture. He came here on his way west to the Gulf of California, thence south until he reached Mexico City. Four centuries later, the bandit leader Pancho Villa routed a federal garrison here during the Mexican Revolution. The survivors, with their families, fled across the river and thence to Marfa on foot, where they were put in boxcars and sent to Fort Bliss, outside El Paso, to be interned until the war was over. Trade between Ojinaga and Presidio was brisk during these years: arms and ammunition were sold to Mexicans, whether federals or rebels, for gold obtained by selling cattle in Presidio which had been taken from dispossessed *hacendados*. General 'Black Jack' Pershing, then commanding US troops at Presidio and setting up cavalry outposts along the river to prevent any incursions from Villa, would later spend a fruitless year in Mexico trying to capture Villa after he invaded US territory at Columbus, New Mexico.

Presidio, so called because of the Spanish military garrison and penal colony established there in the eighteenth century, is today in the business of growing melons, onions and alfalfa. Its population increase, from 1,000 in 1970 to 5,000 at the end of the century, was almost entirely Mexican, many of them formerly illegal immigrants who were amnestied or otherwise absorbed into the Texan border community. But it is in no way a thriving community: in 2000 there was forty per cent unemployment and the average per capita income was said to be $4,000, with half of all families in Presidio living below the poverty line. Most of the work is seasonal, and after the cantaloupe crop had been devastated by whitefly in 2000, it was expected to become more part-time. Ojinaga is a more agreeable place than Presidio, less obviously spoilt than other border towns, with a pretty *zocalo* (central square) and white stuccoed church. (The Chihuahua Pacifico Railroad, through Copper Canyon to the Pacific Ocean, is said to begin in Ojinaga, but the passenger service starts only in Chihuahua city.)

On the American bank, going north, a few villages face each other across the river, but beyond Candelaria, which has about fifty inhabitants, and its opposite Chihuahua number, San Antonio del Bravo, there are no paved roads or settled habitations on the Texas side for the next hundred miles. The railway line stays east of the Sierra Vieja mountain range, and as the sun set behind Eagle Mountain it was announced that we were crossing the border into the Mountain Standard Time zone. Since our train was by now about six hours behind schedule, this information seemed somewhat academic. The railway comes back to the river alongside Highway 10 and runs past two seventeenth-century missions and through the sprawling outskirts of El Paso to its downtown Union station. My train journey would end here, but Amtrak's Sunset Limited service would continue through New Mexico, Arizona and California, due in Los Angeles the following morning. No one was betting it would get there before nightfall.

El Paso's station hall is a great deal larger and more imposing than Houston's run-down waiting-room. It has a tiled floor, ceiling fans and a balustraded balcony above. This is entirely appropriate to El Paso's importance (past more than present) as a railway terminus. Nowadays the traffic is all freight, except for the thrice-weekly passenger service; but a notice from 1910 lists eight different rail companies serving El Paso. Their names, evocative of historic pioneering journeys of the nineteenth century, are worth recording: the Atchison, Topeka & Santa Fe; the El Paso & South-Western; the Chicago, Rock Island & El Paso; the Galveston, Harrisburg & San Antonio; the Mexican Central; the Texas & Pacific; the Southern Pacific; the Rio Grande, Sierra Madre & Pacific. During the first years of the century more than a third of El Paso's factory workforce was employed in railway-car shops. The city's population was then around forty thousand, having jumped from a few hundred in 1880, the year before the railway came to El Paso. But the history of El Paso del Rio del Norte goes back to the sixteenth century.

Spanish conquistadors came north around 1580, and by the end of the century a Mexican-born Creole, Juan de Oñate, had founded the province of New Mexico and begun to colonise the area at the head of the Pass of the North. Coming up from Mexico City, he took the route which, as it became well worn, would be known as the Camino Real, and reached the Rio Grande where it flows almost at the foot of the

Franklin Mountains, the most southerly tip of the Rocky Mountain chain. Sixty years later the first Spanish-Indian settlement was founded at what is now Ciudad Juárez, on the south bank of the river.

In one of the main squares of downtown El Paso I found a statue of Fray García de San Francisco y Zuniga, who is credited with building the settlement's first mission church, to serve the Mansos Indians. He is looking towards the city across the river where he lived and which in his time was known as El Paso del Norte. It took the name of President Benito Juárez in 1888, commemorating the period in 1865–67 when Juárez retreated here and established a government-in-exile during the brief reign of Emperor Maximilian. An oddly romantic dedication is inscribed on the plinth of Fray García's statue: 'To voyagers, passers through, troubadours, foragers crafting a world from sand, granite and limited waters.' It is also rather puzzling: the man who is commemorated here did his crafting in Mexico, where the only statue to him is a small replica of the one in El Paso. It stands outside his mission church, and was given by the city of El Paso to the city of Juárez in 1994 – shaming the citizens of Juárez, one hopes, for having failed to give proper recognition to their founder. For it is here in Juárez that Fray García left his mark; he left no buildings, no record of a settlement on the north bank of the river, and there is no reason for him to be remembered in what is now the United States. That he is serves as a reminder of the close association between these two border cities, which today have a combined population of almost two million. What Juárez may perhaps be proud of is its monument to Abraham Lincoln, the only one outside the United States.

A statue of Christ stands on a peak above the border where Texas, Chihuahua and New Mexico meet, seeming to embrace as one the two communities lying beneath the Mexican dust and the tall stacks of the American Smelting and Refining Company. Maps of El Paso extend south of the river to include the main streets and attractions of Juárez;

and the El Paso–Juárez Trolley Company runs hourly tours from the United States with shopping and restaurant stops in Mexico. In Santa Fé Street, a few hundred yards north of the bridge, a shop window is filled with icons of the Virgin of Guadalupe, Mexico's patron saint. In El Paso's Museum of Art, on the other side of the square from Fray García's statue, I was interested to note that the Juárez newspaper, *El Diario*, is listed as one of the museum's principal benefactors. What makes this the more surprising is that the great majority of paintings in the museum are European (very few of them Spanish) and contemporary American. (One exception is the work of José Cisneros, who was still living in El Paso, in his eighties, at the turn of the century, and still sketching figures from borderlands history.)

Juárez has its own Museo de Arte, but I didn't get there. After walking across the international bridge on a blisteringly hot August day and then another half-mile to Fray García's mission church of Nuestra Señora de Guadalupe, I had almost had enough. Its white façade stands next to, and is dwarfed by, the twin towers of the neo-classical cathedral in the Avenida 16 de Septiembre (Independence Day). Both are impressive, standing at the end of a broad avenue, but the rest of the centre of Ciudad Juárez is decidedly not. I walked down main streets which were dug up for the laying of electricity cables and water pipes – necessary work, no doubt, but they were still not going to serve the electricity- and water-free *colonias* on the outskirts of the city. Seedy-looking dental clinics and pharmacies are commonly seen, next to run-down hotels with peeling plaster and pock-marked walls – one called Hotel Diamante with Hollywood Club Live Girls on the ground floor – which looked as if they had been casualties of a Mexican shoot-out. A few signs brought a wry smile: the Calle Gardenias, in which none of the smells were fragrant; a Taurus Unisex hairdresser, doing business beneath the stands of the city bullring; and a pharmacy poster urging me to 'Spice up your Wife/Life with Viagra'. The only haven to be found was a restaurant, Nuevo Martinos, cooled by large ceiling fans and offering margaritas and *cabrito*, reminiscent of a similar oasis in Nuevo Laredo. After lunch my wife and I walked back across the bridge roofed over with an arch of strong-mesh wire. A US Customs officer on the other side looked at our passports and said: 'You from England? What the hell you think you're doing in a place like this?'

It was a fair question. He was presumably referring to the city's reputation as the headquarters of the most infamous and violent drugs cartel along the border, which sometimes literally liquidates its victims in drums of acid, or cuts off their index fingers and stuffs them in their mouths before shooting them in the back of the head. The customs officer was also no doubt thinking of the hundreds of thousands who live in slum suburbs like Anapra, close to the US border, and who – most of them women – work in the three hundred and twenty-five assembly plants (*maquiladoras*) in the city. After hours the more desperate offer sex in exchange for cocaine and heroin. The Border Industrialization Program, which created the *maquiladoras* in the mid-1960s, began as the brainchild of Antonio J. Bermudez, who wanted to find a way of attracting US investment to Juárez. Now he has the largest border industrial park named after him. While the *maquilas* may have provided a job of sorts, they have also brought squalor and crime to the border towns, from which there seems to be no escape. The only way out, for the *maquila* workers as for the huge numbers of unemployed from the interior who have swelled the populations of Juárez and elsewhere on the border, is to move on north, illegally, to the United States.

Without sanitation in the shanty-town *colonias*, and with pollution caused by dust, chemical run-off and toxic smoke, it is hardly surprising that infant mortality rates are so high and disease rife. There was an outbreak of cholera in Juárez in 1993, and tuberculosis and polio are common. Water is so scarce that people die every summer of dysentery and dehydration. Many *maquila* workers spend a proportion of their meagre salaries in the pharmacies, where they resort to drugs banned in the United States yet widely available across the border without prescription – and without any warning of their side-effects. Pyrazolone, for example, is an addictive analgesic which can damage kidneys and suppress bone marrow. Lincomycin is an antibiotic which may attack stomach and intestinal linings. None of these evils, of course, is exclusive to Ciudad Juárez; but all the miseries associated with border towns seem to be writ larger here. With a population increasing by some fifty thousand a year, Juárez is said to be running out of water. In the poorest *colonias*, you are told, the year begins with fires and gas explosions as people try to keep warm. In spring, they fight for ground on which to build shacks, and in summer, they suffer from disease and lack of water. Autumn is the time of year for the violent settling of accounts and for suicides. And then there is the trade in illegal drugs.

South of the city, four mass graves were discovered in November 1999, said to contain over a hundred victims of the drugs trade (some of them American citizens). One grave was uncovered close to a shooting range, at a place known as Hidden Treasure Ranch. The investigation was notable for the fact that it was kept away from the local police, because some of them would have passed warnings to their paymasters, the drugs barons. The FBI joined the federal Mexican police and military authorities (also possibly on the payrolls of the drug cartels) in trying to identify the murdered and trace the murderers; and the traffic in Colombian cocaine and heroin across the Rio Grande was quite unaffected.

There is a saying about Ciudad Juárez that 'even the Devil would be frightened to live there'. A US counter-intelligence expert assisting the federal police in the city vanished, with his wife, in 1994. They were never heard of again. Juárez is notorious also for other 'disappeared ones'. They are not victims of the drugs trade or of political repression, but teenage girls who go missing and whose bodies, or remains, may be found months later in the Lote Bravo, a desert area outside the city. Most of them are *maquiladora* workers, some working in bars during their spare time; and the police are not interested. The lives of poor women in Juárez have no value: they may or may not be supplementing their income by prostitution, but they are at risk every time they walk, often at night through unlit streets, to and from their jobs on the *maquiladora* assembly lines. Their earnings give them a degree of independence which their mothers would not have enjoyed. But it does not bring them respect: machismo is still going strong in Mexico, and a woman resists a man at her peril.

A member of a Mexican feminist group has said, 'If you want to rape and kill a woman, there is no better place to do it than in Juárez.' By the mid-1990s, the number of victims being found in the Lote Bravo was such that an outcry forced the police to do something. What they did was to arrest an Egyptian chemist and announce that he was the serial killer of all these unfortunate young women. But the killings went on while he languished in jail beginning a thirty-year sentence; though his conviction was later overturned, he was not released. The police shrugged their shoulders, then bestirred themselves a year later and arrested members of a gang called Los Rebeldes, who were convicted of thirteen murders. When the murder rate for young women continued to rise, the police blamed the Egyptian for masterminding the crime wave from his prison cell, where he remained beyond 2000. On the walls of government buildings you may see posters asking, 'Where are our daughters Griselda and Silvia?' and pleading, 'Help us to find Maria.' When the police are not holding the Egyptian responsible, they excuse themselves by claiming that most of these girls have brought it on themselves by dressing provocatively or going out with *narcotraficantes*. After all, this is a dangerous town, with drug-dealing gangs maintaining a culture of violence. What can an honest policeman do when rival drugs traffickers shoot each other in public restaurants and the head of the country's anti-drugs police, a General Jesus Gutierrez Rebollo, was arrested (in 1997) for being on the Juárez drugs cartel's payroll? If a policeman is approached by a member of the cartel, it is simply a question, they say, of *plata o plomo*, silver or lead. You either take the bribe or you get the bullet.

Heading north one day by bus from Chihuahua to Juárez, we followed the old route of the Camino Real, with a range of hills always to left and right. The burnt and arid landscape, dotted with scrub, would scarcely have changed over the centuries since those intrepid Spaniards trekked towards the Pass of the North between the two great mountain chains. But there are also occasional fields of green grazed by cattle destined for the American market, on grass specially sown and kept watered by huge mechanised sprinklers. A large expanse of sand-dunes not far from Juárez is presumably the site of the burial grounds one hears about, containing the corpses of abused women and victims of the drugs trade.

Then we came to a prominent road sign – 'Bienvenidos a Ciudad Juárez; La Mejor Frontera de Mexico'. It was hard to believe this was not a Mexican joke. The best frontier for whom? For drug-dealers and immigrants? The flat-roofed sprawl stretching far into the distance and the vast number of abandoned cars piled high in roadside scrapyards testify to the fact that Juárez is a dump, not least for the vast majority of the 1.8 million unfortunates who live there. The scale of violence and corruption in the city is such that the mayor has more than once had to consider calling in the army to maintain order. At the international bridge a man proffered a collecting tin for the Missionary Church of the Disciples of Jesus Christ. It was for the suffering citizens of Juárez, he said, especially the young drug addicts who could buy heroin produced in Sinaloa at fatally low prices. At the Camino Real Hotel in El Paso, I looked from an upstairs window across the border to Juárez and the mountains behind, the most northerly extremity of the Sierra

Madre. On the side of one hill overlooking the city there is inscribed in huge letters, 'La Biblia es la verdad. LEELA.' ('The Bible is the truth. READ IT.') Even those poor people of Juárez who are able to read may wonder how the Bible can help to alleviate their lot.

El Paso and Juárez are the Cities of the Pass, sharing a watershed in a plain between two mountain ranges, Even from the air, however, it is not hard to tell the two apart. The tall office blocks of downtown El Paso are not to be found south of the river; nor are the neat rows of well-built Texan houses with cypresses standing sentinel beside them. The Rio Grande provides the narrowest of borders here, having been canalised in the 1960s, after the river had changed its course many years earlier during a period of flooding, effectively transferring to the United States a piece of land which had previously been Mexican territory. It was not until 1962, when President Kennedy was seeking Latin American support during the Cuban missile crisis, that a settlement of this border question in Mexico's favour was offered. A large number of people and a few bridges had to be moved before the two presidents, Lyndon Johnson and Gustavo Díaz Ordaz, met on the border in 1967 to agree the Chamizal settlement, and the making of a canal to ensure that the border would not move again.

El Centauro del Norte

Chapter Five

Pancho Villa Rides Again

I SAT in the bar of the Camino Real Hotel, beneath a magnificent coloured-glass dome designed by Louis Tiffany, waiting for the US Border Patrol guard, son of one of my fleeting acquaintances on the train from Houston, whom I had met briefly at the station in El Paso. He had given me a lift in his pick-up, and we had arranged to meet two days later in the Tiffany Dome bar. He had already told me that the situation in the El Paso sector, despite the official line, was getting steadily worse – more drugs and more wetbacks coming across – and I looked forward to hearing about his own experiences. But he never showed up. Perhaps he was out chasing *indocumentados* in the hills or – more likely – he had had second thoughts about talking to an inquisitive writer. That day's Juárez newspaper, *El Diario*, carried a report from El Paso (it was the lead story on the front page) on new regulations for US Customs officers to restrain their persistent abuse of Mexicans suspected of smuggling drugs. Measures were being introduced to limit body searches and ensure that travellers entering the United States were treated courteously and not subjected to racial prejudice. I turned to the *El Paso Times* to see what it had to say about this, but it didn't rate a mention. The paper reported instead that Barry McCaffrey, the anti-drugs 'czar' who had just been visiting El Paso and Juárez, considered it likely that the majority of drug trafficking across the border would be brought to an end within five years. That could be politely described as wildly optimistic.

❧ Pancho Villa Rides Again ❦

In El Paso it is a relief to be able to recall the days of old-fashioned frontier violence, unrelated to drugs, when the *pistoleros* who frequently shot one another were surely not as ruthless and unpleasant as today's gunmen from the drug cartels. In the Concordia Cemetery some of El Paso's most notorious sons have been laid to rest, including John Wesley Hardin who killed at least thirty before being shot dead himself. There is a well-known ballad which tells of a cowboy shooting dead a rival for the hand of Felina, a dancer in Rosa's Cantina, then stealing a horse and riding 'just as fast as I could from the West Texas town of El Paso / Out to the badlands of Old Mexico'. But he comes back across the border to see Felina again, and as he approaches Rosa's bar in El Paso is surrounded by a posse.

> I see a white puff of smoke from the rifle,
> I feel the bullet go deep in my chest.
> From out of nowhere Felina has found me,
> Kissing my cheek as she kneels by my side.
> Cradled by two loving arms that I'll die for,
> One little kiss and Felina goodbye.

Was it all so much simpler in those days? In the Camino Real Hotel I was reminded of the badlands of Old Mexico when passing a conference room named Pancho Villa. But he was no simple *bandido* dealing in a little contraband and death along the border. He was a revolutionary who invaded the United States and got caught up in the First World War.

A photograph I have of Villa shows an open, simple peasant face — possibly a chile short of an *enchilada* — and a burly physique. He is wearing a buttoned striped shirt over a vest, a crumpled suit with waistcoat and watch-chain and a wide-brimmed hat on the back of his head. He has rather a jaunty air — he was said to love dancing — but he had a famously short temper. One might not suppose from the photographs that he had been guilty of so much callous – and casual – cruelty, habitually shooting both civilians and prisoners. But an American journalist who knew him described his eyes as 'never still and full of energy and brutality; intelligent as hell and as merciless'. Born Doroteo Arango in the state of Durango, he took his grandfather's name of Villa as a teenager and embarked on a life of banditry. He moved his base of operations to Chihuahua around the turn of the century, where he rustled cattle, robbed and ransacked with a bloodthirsty gang of fellow thieves. He had certainly committed murder several times – including the shooting of a former comrade in one of the main streets of Chihuahua city – by the time he met Francisco Madero, who told him that his sins could be redeemed by joining the Army of Liberation to get rid of the elderly dictator, Porfirio Díaz, whose thirty-five-year rule was accordingly brought to an end in May 1911.

At the point where the border leaves the Rio Grande and becomes a fence going west through brush-covered hills, a white obelisk records the start of the Mexican Revolution, the first revolution of the twentiethth century. (The uprising had in fact begun the previous November, when Madero issued his first rallying cry from the Texas border.) Once Madero, with Villa's and Pascual Orozco's irregulars, had taken Ciudad Juárez, using dynamite which became the most popular weapon of the revolution, he signed articles of peace conditional upon Díaz going into exile. Then he advanced south to Mexico City, promising 'Tierra y Libertad' (Land and Liberty). His arrival in the capital coincided with a massive earthquake. Villa remained in the north, where he enjoyed being compared to Robin Hood. Orozco took control of the state of Chihuahua, then lost it to the federal army general, Victoriano Huerta, who was joined by Villa, returning to the colours after a period of rest and relaxation, in which he ran butchers' shops in the north and started on a career of serial polygamy, which his subsequent military campaigns never seemed to interrupt. Once Chihuahua had been retaken, Huerta ordered Villa to be shot when he said he would take his forces, now known as the Division del Norte, off on his own. He avoided the firing squad at least twice, reached Mexico City and was imprisoned. Having escaped and made his way to El Paso, where newspaper reporters were usually able to track him down in an ice-cream parlour, he returned after Madero's assassination in 1913 to re-form the Division del Norte, and had soon made himself master of the state of Chihuahua. He also decided it was time he became a film star and signed a contract with the US Mutual Film Corporation, agreeing to fight his battles by day and delay his executions until after dawn to assist the cameramen. *The Life of General Villa* opened in New York in May 1914, with the hero becoming president of Mexico as a 'happy ending' to the film.

He was less popular in England at this time, having just shot dead a British citizen and ranch owner, William Benton, in a dispute over grazing rights and the looting of his property by Villa's troops. 'Englishman foully murdered in Mexico' was the headline in one newspaper. Questions were asked in the House of Commons and comparisons made with Jenkins's ear and Don Pacifico. But on this occasion Britain was prevented from mobilising her ships and troops by respect for the Monroe Doctrine. Without its constraints, the US ambassador in London wrote to President Wilson, 'they would India-ize and Egypt-ize Mexico for ever'. The foreign secretary, Sir Edward Grey, admitted rather lamely that the government could do nothing except ask the president to bring his influence to bear. But Wilson was pursuing his policy of 'watchful waiting', which didn't really help to avenge Benton's murder. In bellicose mood, *The Spectator* declared that the Monroe Doctrine carried an obligation on the part of the United States to do everything possible to protect the lives and property of Europeans in Latin America. 'It is not to be supposed that British citizens may be freely assassinated without any satisfaction being sought.' US military intervention was inevitable, *The Spectator* opined, and the sooner the better. But Wilson's intervention consisted of little more than asking Villa for an explanation and demanding the release of Benton's body for examination, which was refused. Villa managed to lie his way out of the incident, initially claiming that Benton had been court-martialled and shot after trying to assassinate him, and suffered no damage to his reputation.

A month later, while the Benton incident was still simmering, Villa carefully avoided any public condemnation of the United States when Wilson ordered the brief occupation by US marines of the port of Veracruz, in an attempt to prevent the delivery of arms and ammunition by a German warship to the government, of which Huerta was now president. It was something of a shambles, with nineteen Americans and a hundred and twenty-six Mexicans killed. The only person to come well out of this episode was an Englishman, Commander Tweedie, who succeeded in evacuating three trainloads of US citizens from Mexico City to the coast.

Huerta, of mostly Indian blood and a serial drinker, did not preside over his country for long. The white-bearded governor of Coahuila, Venustiano Carranza, established a 'constitutionalist' government in the north and it was one of his lieutenants, Alvaro Obregón, a former chickpea farmer and poker player (and future president), who was first into Mexico City in August 1914, following Huerta's resignation. Villa got there in December, having won notable, and very bloody, battles at Torreon and Zacatecas on the way. He had his famous meeting with Emiliano Zapata – when the khaki uniforms of his followers contrasted oddly with the white pyjamas of the Zapatistas – but their intended alliance was stillborn. For a brief period towards the end of that year, Villa appeared to have the capital under his control or, rather, reign of terror. At all events, he was the only one of the Big Four – Carranza,

Obregón, Zapata, Villa – in Mexico City when the Japanese commander of a visiting warship, who was also an envoy of his government, came to call on the man in charge; and it was Villa whom he sought out and to whom he addressed a critical question. What would be Mexico's position in the event of war between Japan and the United States?

It is extraordinary to recall how this bandit revolutionary got caught up in the power politics of the First World War. In the early months of the war, President Woodrow Wilson looked favourably on Villa for having opposed Huerta's rule, and he now seemed to Wilson capable of providing an alternative to the chaos over which Carranza was ineffectively presiding. (Carranza was also implacably anti-gringo.) So Villa deemed it politic to tell the envoy from Japan that his country's forces would not be deployed against its northern neighbour in the event that the United States became embroiled in war.

When Huerta was ousted, a German ship took him to exile in Spain, and it was Germany that brought him back the following spring. He disembarked in New York, where it was made clear to him that Germany would back a military coup to restore him to power. The idea was to provoke Wilson to go blundering once again into another Veracruz, leading to a war with Mexico which would stop the flow of American munitions to the Allies and distract Wilson's attention from the European theatre. Huerta took a train to San Francisco, then changed in Kansas City for Texas, where he was to be met by his old enemy Orozco and taken across the border to resume command of forces still loyal to him. But he was arrested instead by a State Department agent when the train stopped at Newman, on the New Mexico–Texas border, and charged with fomenting rebellion. In El Paso, to the State Department's embarrassment, Huerta was greeted with enthusiasm and the town's mayor offered to act as his attorney. Across the river in Ciudad Juárez, the military garrison and several thousand mercenaries were waiting to rally to him. The US Army was understandably anxious to get Huerta away from the border, and prevailed upon him to go to Fort Bliss, a few miles into the Texas hinterland, where he was later held in custody. The excitement died down, Huerta's health deteriorated, and in January 1916, to the accompaniment of sighs of relief in Washington, he died. (Rumours that the US army was responsible for hastening Huerta's demise were never substantiated.)

Pancho Villa, meanwhile, had spent most of 1915 making fatal mistakes. He lost the civil war, he lost his power base and he lost the support of the United States. Time and again he rejected the advice of his best general and tactical adviser, Felipe Angeles, to withdraw in order to stretch the enemy's lines of communication. Instead he insisted on making wild and unsupported cavalry charges at every opportunity. Villa also took his fight against Carranza to Tamaulipas. He sent a 15,000-strong army on an abortive attempt to capture Tampico, and 3,000 troops to besiege Matamoros. Though repulsed, Villa scored a first when his men fired on a US military plane. His jacket, spurs and cartridge belt are exhibited in the old Fort Casamata in Matamoros, but it is doubtful if he was present at the battle. He was, meanwhile, in danger of losing control of northern Mexico. The United States had recognised Carranza, effectively ditching Villa, and made it possible for government forces in the north to bring reinforcements through southern New Mexico and Arizona to defeat Villa at the battle of Agua Prieta. Villa, brooding in his winter quarters, decided that Washington was resolved to make Mexico its colony; it was time to teach that gringo president a lesson. In the same week that Huerta died, a band of Villistas waylaid a train at Santa Ysabel in the province of Chihuahua and shot dead eighteen of its passengers, all of them American mining engineers. In the ensuing furore, ex-president Theodore Roosevelt called for the army to march into Mexico immediately; but Wilson more sagely was determined to do all he could to avoid war. Armed conflict with Mexico was just what Germany was trying to provoke, and to that end gave encouragement both to Villa and to Carranza. There were reports of German businessmen congregating in El Paso and German officers being seen along the border.

Through banks in El Paso, it was said that nearly a million dollars was transferred from Germany to Mexican troops. A German agent apparently joined Villa's staff and told him that the state bank in the border town of Columbus, New Mexico, had cheated Villa out of ten thousand dollars. Villa responded as he was supposed to and, exactly two months after Santa Ysabel, sent several hundred of his horsemen at night across the international border and into Columbus, killing another eighteen US citizens – and losing about a hundred of his own men. Villa himself apparently stayed on the Mexican side of the border with reserve troops who repelled the American pursuit when the raiders returned. Some called Villa's invasion of American territory his *delirio de grandeza*; others said he was merely doing Germany's bidding by keeping the United States occupied with the provocations of its neighbour. It was even said that Washington knew of Villa's intentions and did nothing to deter him. In the somewhat tortuous logic behind this theory, Wilson, while determined to keep his country out of the European war and putting himself forward as the peace candidate in the presidential elections later that year, needed an excuse to increase the strength of the US armed forces, which were in no way comparable to military numbers in Europe.

In any event, Wilson felt obliged to react to this incursion into US territory. With Carranza's consent, he dispatched General 'Black Jack' Pershing to Mexico with a force of some ten thousand, 'for the sole purpose of capturing the bandit Villa'. (A recruiting poster appealed for 25,000 men, 'necessary to raise the US Army to War Strength ... Come on boys: Be ready to shoulder the trusty Springfield.') In this enterprise the US army was completely unsuccessful, in spite of offering a five-thousand-dollar reward for delivering Villa dead or alive. His reputation as a guerrilla leader recovered, and he went on marauding at will, even retaking the state capital and Torreon. But he lost popular support when he authorised the shooting of ninety women suspected of consorting with Carranza's troops.

Pershing floundered around northern Mexico for the best part of a year without ever setting eyes on Villa, though his troops were sometimes fired on by Villa's or by Carranza's forces. At one stage, the entire National Guard of fifty thousand men was dispatched to the border towns of El Paso, Brownsville and Nogales after some twenty US cavalrymen had been taken prisoner at Carrizal, in the desert south of Ciudad Juárez. Eight biplanes were assigned to Pershing, the first exercise in US military air power, but they soon broke down and were of no further use to him. Eventually, as this fruitless intrusion into a foreign country became increasingly embarrassing, the United States was obliged to withdraw from what was called its punitive expedition, in which nobody had been punished. Germany was disappointed that nothing more than one or two brief clashes between American and Mexican troops had taken place. However, the Imperial German Minister in Mexico, von Eckhardt, was now getting on very well with Carranza – which was crucial to the Kaiser's Mexican plan.

Germany's interest in Mexico went back to the beginning of the century, when the Kaiser initiated legal moves in London in order to try and purchase a stretch of the southern peninsula of Baja California. Magdalena Bay was the place the Kaiser wanted – it has a large natural harbour suitable as a naval base. Japan was interested too, and a few years later, according to rumour, was about to lease it from the Mexican government. Neither country acquired a foothold on Mexico's Pacific coast, but both had at least put out feelers. Japan talked about the Mexicans, however improbably, as their racial brothers, descended from Japanese fishermen who had crossed the Pacific thousands of years before. When Admiral Yashiro paid a state visit to Mexico in 1911, he made a speech referring to the same blood flowing in Japanese and Mexican veins and the need to make common cause against the common enemy. At a time when America had imposed restrictions on the entry of Japanese labour and, in its initial revolutionary fervour, Mexico was getting worked up again over the loss of its former territories (1848 was not so long ago), there was no doubt as to the identity of the common enemy. 'Abajo los gringos! Viva Japon!' were the cries heard in Mexico City not only by Admiral Yashiro but by American observers of his visit.

Rumour soon spread of a secret treaty between Japan and Mexico; President Taft mobilised twenty thousand troops (two thirds of the US regular army) on the Mexican border, and sent the fleet to the Gulf of Mexico. War with Japan was surely imminent: a New York newspaper claimed to have evidence not only that a treaty existed between Mexico and Japan but that Taft had seen it. Suspicious-looking Orientals had been sighted in Mexican border towns, and the US Army was expected in Mexico City by Easter. But none of it was true. Taft had mobilised American forces because of the threat to American business interests in Mexico from the insurrection which was about to depose President Díaz. And the story of a treaty was fed to the newspaper by the German military attaché in Washington. The fact that so many believed it, however, gave the Kaiser another idea.

In letters to his cousin Nicholas, Czar of all the Russias, Kaiser Wilhelm sympathised with his defeat at the hands of the Japanese in 1904–05, referring to this formidable race, possibly the first to do so, as the Yellow Peril. But, having reflected for a year or two, the Kaiser came to see these Prussians of the East as Germany's potential allies, together with Mexico, against the United States. In his bizarre but fertile *Weltanschauung*, the Kaiser envisaged Japan seizing the recently built Panama Canal and America losing its domination of the rest of Latin

America. Japanese forces would then move north into friendly Mexico, and the United States would be compelled to invade its southern neighbour. England would have to back America, depriving her of her then Japanese ally. Initially the Kaiser was urging President Roosevelt to action to defeat the Yellow Peril, but by 1916 the war in Europe dictated another tactic. The German military commanders had persuaded themselves that the unrestricted use of U-boats against all enemy and neutral shipping would force Britain's surrender within six months, before America had had time to organise and transport an army across the Atlantic. (A major part of its regular army was still chasing around northern Mexico in vain pursuit of Pancho Villa.) The use of bases on the Mexican coast would be very helpful to the U-boats; and a military alliance between Germany and Mexico could be used to persuade President Carranza to invade the USA in the event that it felt obliged, by continued attacks on its shipping, to enter the war against Germany. It had not, of course, escaped Germany's notice that Carranza was now also on good terms with Japan.

Following regular invitations to the Japanese ambassador to dine at the presidential palace, a Mexican army officer sailed in November 1916 for Tokyo, where he arranged to buy large quantities of arms and the equipment to build an ammunition factory in Mexico, together with Japanese personnel to operate it. In the same month, Germany appointed a new foreign minister, Arthur Zimmermann, who thought the time was right for persuading Mexico, with Japan's assistance, to take up arms against the United States. Whether or not Mexico was capable of mobilising a cohesive force for this purpose – throughout 1916 the country's revolution had been bloodier than ever – Herr Zimmermann decided to put forward the proposal that would finally force an extremely reluctant Woodrow Wilson into the war with Germany which he had spent most of his presidency trying to avoid.

President Wilson's re-election in 1916 had been largely due to his success in keeping America out of the war in Europe and his promise to continue to distance his country from war. He talked of negotiating 'peace without victory' between the Allies and Germany, which was of interest to neither side. Britain, now in grave danger of being defeated, despaired of Wilson's ever agreeing to enter the war against Germany. But then, on 16 January 1917, the German foreign secretary sent a telegram to his ambassador in Washington, to be passed on to his minister in Mexico. When it was first intercepted and decoded in London, the British foreign secretary, Arthur Balfour, knew it could be the answer to Britain's prayers. For what Zimmermann was proposing was an offensive alliance with Mexico – 'make war together, make peace together' – and 'an understanding on our part that Mexico is to reconquer the lost territory in Texas, New Mexico and Arizona'. He added the suggestion that Carranza should sound out Japan with a view to drawing her into the alliance. This really was dynamite. When the usually languorous Balfour handed the text of the Zimmermann telegram to the American ambassador in London, he described it as 'the most dramatic moment in all my life'. And when it was published the American press and people, under direct threat now from three countries, and fearing invasion from the Pacific and across the Rio Grande, were almost unanimous in deciding that their neutrality must be brought to an end. In the Midwest, even German Americans and America's German-language newspapers were obliged to take a stand against this dastardly Prussian invasion plot. As a first step, America armed its merchant ships against the unrestricted U-boat war launched on 1 February.

German officials and agents were meanwhile to be observed in Mexico, inspecting its railways and military bases, landing consignments of arms at Mexican ports and generally stirring up trouble. In the north, Pancho Villa got the message and left German-owned stores and warehouses alone when he went on his rampages through the state of

Chihuahua. And while he continued to keep his whereabouts secret from General Pershing and a large part of the US Army still searching for him, it was said that the German consul in Juárez always knew where Villa was to be found. That damned elusive bandit told his army of irregulars they would help the Germans beat the United States and then be able to reclaim their lost territories. A US federal agent reported from El Paso: 'My men on track of big German–Villa combination.' But it came to nothing. President Carranza was embarrassed by disclosure of the alliance proposal, and by the fact that several Latin American countries, including Mexico's neighbour, Guatemala, had broken off relations with Germany. He was also busy establishing a new constitution for his country, and he became slightly less hostile to the United States when, in the first week of February 1917, Pershing admitted defeat – he had been trying to find Villa for the best part of a year – and withdrew his forces from Mexico. By the time, in mid-April, that Carranza communicated to Zimmermann his decision to remain neutral, America had declared war on Germany and Pershing was soon leading his troops across the Atlantic, where they were to enjoy greater success than in the Mexican desert.

Villa was undeterred: he went on with his guerrilla activities for another three years, until Carranza was assassinated and succeeded as president by another of the original revolutionary leaders, Alvaro Obregón (who was himself murdered in 1928). Villa was given an estate at Canutillo, south of Hidalgo del Parral, where he lived with a bodyguard of fifty armed men. But in 1923, at the age of forty-five, he suffered the fate of almost all Mexican leaders of the time, except that he was killed after he had retired. It was early in the morning of 20 July, as he was being driven in his new black Dodge through Parral after visiting one of his mistresses, that General Villa was shot dead at a street corner in a hail of bullets. President Obregón, who had once faced death from Villa's firing squad, was almost certainly behind the murder.

And he was probably egged on by Plutarco Calles, who was to become president the following year and feared that Villa might make a comeback and deny him the succession.

In El Paso's Camino Real Hotel I was told that, in addition to Pancho Villa, General Pershing and President Taft had both stayed there during those turbulent years. But Villa is the only one to have a hotel function room named after him. It is an enjoyable irony that a man who invaded the United States, killed a number of its citizens, and colluded with the country which was about to become America's enemy, should be commemorated in this way in Texas. Yet Pancho Villa was a legendary figure in these parts, and he was fighting for land and freedom for his people. Or was he rather fighting for himself and his band of bloodthirsty followers? Either way, I think he deserves a room in El Paso's best hotel.

Villa's reputation lived on through his widow, Luz Corral. (She was, at any rate, his 'number one' wife, though there were several subsequent mistresses with whom he contracted bogus marriages.) She became something of a public figure over the next sixty years and did not die until 1982, aged ninety. She entertained Mexican presidents at the Villa home in Chihuahua – she had cleverly obtained a pension for herself from Obregón – and travelled often to California, being welcomed by mayors and film stars. She received a papal blessing and even had a poem written to her by Eileen Rockefeller, who expressed her admiration not only for a brave woman but for the 'heroic' husband who was never arraigned for his crimes.

> Where others would have died of grief
> You live.
> Where others would have shrunk from publicity
> You ask us in.
> And where others would have fallen apart

❧ Pancho Villa Rides Again ❦

> You picked up the pieces
> To teach us of the hero
> You lived so long without.
> Listening to you we learn
> The meaning of courage.

Today the Villa house in Chihuahua is open to visitors. It stands in a quiet road, looking past cypresses towards the brown hills, harsh and barren, of Pancho Villa's country. Though Villa himself may not have lived here, it is still a surprise to find that his wife, to whom he was married throughout the years of revolution, chose for herself a formal town house. It is a fine stone building with balustrades, elaborate lintels over the windows and a first-floor balcony above the imposing pillared porch. Inside, a gallery encircles an open courtyard, with fountain and an orange tree. A few minutes' walk away, in this most attractive of northern Mexican cities, a stunning Art Nouveau house, built in the first decade of the twentieth century, was used for a while by Villa as his barracks.

The Villa Villa reveals something of the general's tastes, if not his character. A number of the painted walls and panels, to be found in almost every room, feature peacocks, which apparently were his favourite bird. The walls of the dining-room, painted by an Italian, have delicate arrangements of fruit against a salmon-pink background. It is not easy to imagine El Valeroso Caudillo de la Revolucion Mexicana dropping in on his wife for dinner in such surroundings after a hard day's or week's work murdering and marauding round his fiefdom. A gaudily painted mural, celebrating the deeds of El Centauro del Norte, is vividly described in an English translation:

> In the center like a ray of ligth Francisco Villa accompagned of his 'golden' scort, wich whirlwind in movement, advance and

eliminating the opresor groups in the power (bourgeoisie and federal army).

The Dodge car, with bullet-holes in the passenger doors, is on display; so is Villa's armoury of repeater rifles, pistols, machine-guns and sabres, mostly made in America and Germany. (His death mask is in a museum in Ciudad Juárez.) In one small room, the walls are adorned with photographs of a proud, moustached line-up of revolutionary generals. One of them, Raul Madero, fought alongside Villa, not only to bring his brother, Francisco Madero, to power in 1911, but during the revolution's later years. He went into exile for a while in the USA, then came out of retirement in the 1950s to be governor of Coahuila. He lived on into his nineties and died in the same year, 1982, as Villa's widow, Luz Corral. It was only then that the Pancho Villa era can be said finally to have ended. Six years earlier, Villa's body was exhumed from its grave in Parral where he was shot and reburied in the Hall of Heroes in Mexico City.

Chapter Six

Desert and the Devil's Road

ONCE THE Mexico–United States border leaves the Rio Grande, it proceeds in straight lines, following treaty rather than topography. Between Old Mexico and New Mexico there is little but desert and a cattle fence. New Mexico, which had been so named by the Spaniards before the end of the sixteenth century, had a short-lived union with Chihuahua in the 1820s as Estado Interno del Norte. Following the surrender of Mexican territory by treaty in 1848, the United States then acquired a further forty-five thousand square miles under the Gadsden Purchase, effectively moving the boundaries of New Mexico, and what became Arizona in 1863, farther south. (This was done primarily in order to facilitate the building of a transcontinental railway.) Neither New Mexico nor Arizona became states of the Union until 1912; only four years earlier New Mexico had voted to join its western neighbour in a single state to be called Arizona, but the people of Arizona voted overwhelmingly against the idea of united statehood.

New Mexico has only three hundred and fifty miles of border with Mexico, and three border posts, one of which, Santa Teresa, is on the outskirts of El Paso and next to one of the largest cattle crossings along the border. The only major road out of El Paso (Highway 10) heads north for a few miles before turning west across the Rio Grande and going all the way to the coast of California. Here, in southern New Mexico, it is all flat, grassy, sandy plain – the real desert comes farther west and south – with stunted mesquite, a few yuccas, swooping birds of prey and distant mountains on either side. Deming is the headquarters of the New Mexico Border Patrol, but the border is thirty miles away, at the village of Columbus, overlooking the three peaks of the Tres Hermanas mountains. Columbus was linked to the El Paso & South-Western railway line at the beginning of the twentieth century, but there was no other reason for anyone to have heard of it until the events of March 1916.

In view of the instability south of the border – Mexico had had four presidents in the previous five years – and the unpredictable activities of Pancho Villa in the adjacent state of Chihuahua, a detachment of the 13th US Cavalry was stationed in Columbus when Villa's horsemen crossed the border one night and ran riot through the town. Today it is odd to find this foreign brigand so celebrated in the town which he did his best to destroy, murdering ten of its residents and eight soldiers. But there are not many other reasons to go there – its permanent population is around seven hundred, smaller than it was in 1916 – and Villa's raid was, after all, the first armed invasion of United States territory since 1812 and the only one in the twentieth century. There is a Pancho Villa State Park, a Pancho Villa Motel, a Pancho Villa Cantina and an International Raid Day Parade, which takes place every 9 March. The Columbus Historical Museum is filled with Villa photographs and Villa memorabilia, and the old US Customs House, now a visitor centre, shows Villa videos. The old US Army camp – the young Lieutenant George Patton was stationed there in 1916, though he had gone off to a polo match in Deming a few hours before the raid – was within what is now the state park. Here you may see thirty different species of cactus and, if you are lucky, a passing snow goose or sandhill crane.

Three miles south, Palomas has a population of several thousand, a handful of *maquiladoras* and tortilla factories, and lots of doves, from which it presumably gets its name. The predominant impression is still

❧ Desert and the Devil's Road ❧

of an old Mexican frontier town: one-storey adobe houses, with strings of red chiles hung in their doorways, and unpaved streets flanked by telegraph poles joined by sagging wires. Relations between the two towns are generally good, and the Columbus fire-engine has been known to go across to Palomas to put out a blaze. At Tillie's restaurant (Palomas also, of course, has a Pancho Villa restaurant), the mayor of Columbus comes to dine and is greeted as 'el presidente'. Cattle go north from Palomas, first being inspected by vets from the US Department of Agriculture and better looked after, so they say, than the two-legged immigrants.

Billy Parham knew this country well from his journeys in *The Crossing*, the second book of Cormac McCarthy's Border Trilogy. His home was Cloverdale, south of Animas and close to Arizona as well as to the Mexican border. On his first ride south, with the wolf, Billy is immediately struck by the fact of being in Mexico:

> ... they crossed sometime near noon the international boundary line into Mexico, state of Sonora, undifferentiated in its terrain from the country they quit and yet wholly alien and wholly strange. He sat the horse and looked out over the red hills. To the east he could see one of the concrete obelisks that stood for a boundary marker. In that desert waste it had the look of some monument to a lost expedition.

McCarthy is good at conveying the harshness and emptiness of this border country of desert and mountain, where Billy occasionally sees

> parties of vaqueros crossing the high grasslands, sometimes mounted on mules for their good footing in the mountains, sometimes driving beeves before them... They crossed in silent defile over the talus slopes and rode up through the passes

toward the high grassy vegas, sitting their horses with their easy formality, the low sun catching the tin cups tied to their saddlehorns. He saw their fires burning on the mountain at night but never did he go to them.

Billy makes a long and dangerous trek through northern Mexico in search of his brother Boyd, whose grave he finally discovers in the town of San Lorenzo, between Juárez and Chihuahua. Billy rides as far south as Cuauhtemoc, then to Namiquipa, 'little more than a mining camp sited on a bluff above the river', which was the home town of many of Villa's Columbus raiders. On his sweep through Chihuahua, General Pershing captured a number of these Villistas in Namiquipa and sent them back for trial in New Mexico, where at least six were subjected to frontier lynch-law justice and hanged. Villa, hearing that some residents of Namiquipa had betrayed the whereabouts of a cache of arms to Pershing, rounded up the young women of the town and let his men rape them.

On one journey south, Billy passes through the only other New Mexico customs post, Antelope Wells, to El Berrendo on the other side. This remote little place – it has no antelope and no wells – is fifty miles from the nearest US town, but it is known to mountain bikers riding the Continental Divide Trail. The mountains here form the Great Divide, with run-off waters falling west towards the Pacific and east to the Gulf of Mexico. When Tom Miller was researching his book *On the Border* in the 1970s, it took him two hours to drive the mostly gravel road south to the border post.

> Had we been sensible we would have turned back after five minutes. No cars passed us in either direction... The only road sign we encountered pointed east into the Big Hatchet Mountains; it said HIGH LONESOME and we believed it.

This is the least used (by humans) port of entry along the entire border; it exists principally as a crossing for cattle. An average of three people a day entered the United States legally at Antelope Wells, Miller wrote, and on the other side El Berrendo consisted of nothing more than two shacks, for customs and immigration. Driving along Highway 10, I saw the turning signposted to Antelope Wells; a narrow, empty road headed south to nowhere. I decided to continue towards Arizona.

The nearest town to El Berrendo is Janos, some thirty miles south, notorious for Apache raids in the nineteenth century and especially as the place where the family of the legendary chief Geronimo was murdered in 1850. For the best part of fifty years, from Sonora to Chihuahua and from Arizona to Texas, the border country was liable to be terrorised by Apache attacks, whether against Mexicans or the US Cavalry. A truce made with one of the twelve divisions of the tribe did not bind the others, so that battles with one Apache chief or another appeared to continue almost without pause. Mexico and the USA, having agreed in the middle of the century the boundaries which the Apaches completely ignored, cooperated for a while to allow each other's troops to cross the border in pursuit of the common enemy. But it was not until General George Crook's expedition into the Sierra Madre in the 1880s that the three principal Indian chiefs, Geronimo, Nana and Juh (who was drowned in the Casas Grandes River), were finally defeated and they and their followers were thereafter confined to reservations. Chihuahua was relatively peaceful for the next twenty-five years, and William Randolph Hearst's seven million acres remained undisturbed. But in a state where war and fighting had become a natural way of life, it was no surprise that this was where the flames of revolution were first rekindled in 1910.

On either side of the New Mexico–Arizona border, the country is dotted with ghost towns – Hachita, Rodeo, Portal – recalling copper-mining days. Near the suitably named town of Apache, a memorial records the surrender of Geronimo in Skeleton Valley in 1886, bringing the Indian wars finally to an end. The first Arizona county adjoining the international boundary, Cochise, is named after a Chiricahua Apache chief. The Chiricahua Mountains, steep-sided and apparently impassable, dominate the skyline, but here in the desert borderland divided by a cattle fence, where Arizona now faces Sonora, the landscape is relentlessly flat. It has not changed since John Russell Bartlett, who led a survey commission in the 1850s to mark the border, wrote of the 'sterile plains, where no tree offered its friendly shade, the sun glowing fiercely, and the wind hot from the parched earth, cracking the lips and burning the earth... As far as the eye can reach stretches one unbroken waste, wild and worthless.'

Agua Prieta (murky water) is the next Mexican border town, with a population, at a hundred and fifteen thousand, almost eight times that of its Arizona neighbour, Douglas. Not much has been heard of Agua Prieta since the revolutionary years, when Pancho Villa made his abortive attack on the town. It was held by a garrison loyal to Venustiano Carranza, whom Woodrow Wilson had recently recognised as the legitimate ruler of Mexico, and had been reinforced by troops permitted to pass through US territory (they travelled by train from El Paso to Douglas). This so infuriated Villa, who felt betrayed by his erstwhile friends, that when asked by an American reporter, 'Will you attack Agua Prieta?' he replied, 'Yes, and the United States if necessary.' In the ensuing battle, which took place at night, Villa was up against General Plutarco Elias Calles (born in Sonora and a future president), who dug trenches and rigged barbed wire against the Villista cavalry, and then used a battery of searchlights against a night infantry attack. Villa was convinced they came from the American side of the border, and within four months he had taken his revenge, by murdering a train-load of US engineers and then, as he had threatened, attacking the United States at its border town of Columbus.

Desert and the Devil's Road

In 1920 a group of Sonorans, including Calles and Alvaro Obregón, drew up their Plan of Agua Prieta (it was signed at one of the town's cafés, owned by an American) for the replacement of President Carranza by an elected successor. Soon afterwards, Carranza fled to Veracruz and was murdered. In the early days of revolution, Francisco Madero had attacked Agua Prieta, but it was soon retaken by Porfirio Díaz's forces, with the citizens of Douglas able to watch the action from a few hundred yards away. In El Paso, too, Texans were often able to enjoy a rooftop view of the progress of the revolution across the river, even if they, and many Mexicans, had little idea of what was going on. These skirmishes so close to the US frontier worried President Taft, who issued a stern warning to both government and rebel forces to keep away, especially where railways crossed the border.

Douglas, founded in 1901, was a copper town, whose smelters were finally closed down and demolished in the late 1980s. After decades of air pollution from the huge smokestacks of the Phelps Dodge Smelter, once described as 'looking like the twin exhaust pipes of hell', Douglas is now a relatively smog-free zone. But when the wind blows from the south, there is still some pollution from the smelter at Cananea, Sonora, fifty miles away, from the dust of the plains and, in winter, from thousands of wood-burning fires in and around Agua Prieta. Douglas's most notable survival today is the Gadsden Hotel which, like the Camino Real Hotel in the border town of El Paso, is adorned with Tiffany stained glass. (Much of the 1970s film, *The Life and Times of Judge Roy Bean* – he who administered the law west of the Pecos from the Texan town of Langtry – was shot at this hotel. Paul Newman and Ava Gardner starred in the film, which was directed by John Huston.)

It is entirely fitting that the Gadsden Hotel should be named after the man who was responsible for Douglas, and much of southern Arizona and New Mexico, belonging to the United States rather than to Mexico. The border established along the Gila River at the end of the Mexican-American War in 1848 left all the copper in Mexico, though of course neither James Gadsden nor anyone else knew this when, five years later, he negotiated on behalf of the USA to buy this desert and mountain territory from Mexico. (Profits from the copper deposits later found in Cananea also accrued to American interests. When Mexican workers went on strike in 1906, the Sonora governor allowed the Arizona Rangers to cross the border to quell what became an armed uprising. The strike leaders were jailed, then released when revolution came five years later.) Douglas's neighbouring mining town of Bisbee was once so wealthy that it was considered a cosmopolitan centre to rival San Francisco; today it houses a colony of artists and musicians and ageing hippies, not unlike Goa.

Relations between Douglas and Agua Prieta have improved in recent years. A Friendship Mission (Mision de Amistad) was founded in 1977 by a retired airforce master sergeant, who started providing food and blankets, particularly at Christmas, for the poor of Agua Prieta. Twenty years later, around 15,000 people a year were benefiting from this distribution and from a drinking-water project funded by corporations and individuals in Arizona. In 1999, for the first time, the twin towns held a joint parade on Mexican Independence Day, 'to highlight the cooperation between the two communities'.

But this is only one side of the relationship. The scale of migration from the south through the Agua Prieta/Douglas sector increased so dramatically at the end of the twentieth century that as many as a thousand undocumented Mexicans, and illegal immigrants of other Central American nationalities, might be tramping every day across Arizona's cattle ranches. The four hundred Border Patrol agents in the Douglas area, using all-terrain vehicles, motor cycles, horses and helicopters, made about twenty thousand arrests a month during 2000; but at least as many were avoiding detection. The Hispanic population of Maricopa County, which includes the capital, Phoenix, more than doubled in the last decade of the century; at least a third of the 1.3 million Hispanics living in the state were thought to have entered illegally. Inevitably, in what may be the busiest stretch of the border between the Gulf and the Pacific, some ranchers do not take kindly to such an invasion of their property. It is bad enough to have illegal aliens crossing their land, but worse when they drop plastic water bottles and bags which choke the cattle.

So-called border vigilantes have been active for years, especially in Arizona. Some, calling themselves the US Patriot Patrol, have been known to shoot at immigrants and beat them up before handing them over to the official Border Patrol service. The Internet has been used by people belonging to groups such as the Ku Klux Klan, who offer for a few hundred dollars 'hunting weekends', where the quarry is human. 'Rabbit-shooting, Mexican-shooting, there ain't a whole lot of difference to those high-dollar, big landowning Republicans in southern Arizona,' I was told. By 2000, the situation had deteriorated to such an extent – more and more immigrants were crossing the border in the less populated areas – that Mexico's former foreign minister protested to Washington at 'racist behaviour that violates all international rules', and the United Nations was asked to investigate human-rights abuses, including immigrant deaths, by US citizens. (Abuses by fellow Mexicans, as the would-be immigrants made their way across their own country, tended to be overlooked.) However, the most notorious case – still talked about in Douglas – occurred in the summer of 1976, when three Mexicans had the misfortune to be spotted one morning by a rancher and his two sons.

George Hanigan had been born on the family homestead in 1909, and still farmed the two thousand acres a little way west of Douglas. He was known as a hard man and he didn't mix with Hispanics. He had founded a right-wing Republican group called Americans for Constitutional Action; but what he did on the day that he apprehended

Manuel, Bernabe and Eleazar was distinctly unconstitutional. There was a time when George's two sons, Tom and Pat, were happy to leave Mexicans alone as they crossed the Hanigan land heading for seasonal jobs in the Sulphur Springs Valley. But one day in 1976 Pat's mobile home was burgled; weapons and jewellery were stolen, and footprints from the trailer went south. The Hanigans resolved that in future wetbacks would cross the ranch at their peril.

Manuel had been working in an orchard north of Douglas until the Border Patrol found him and took him back to Mexico. Bernabe, aged eighteen, had been on the road for two years, crossing the border many times in search of the 'stoop labour' that Americans did their best to avoid. Eleazar had worked for two years at an American-owned textile plant in Agua Prieta, but when he lost his job he began crossing the line for a few weeks at a time to weed cotton fields, regularly returning home to his wife and three-month-old son.

On this day the three Mexicans were subjected to a citizens' arrest, Hanigan-style. They had their hands tied with rope and were told to lie on the ground. Their ankles were tied, their clothes cut from them with knives, and the small sums of money they were carrying were taken. Then a fire was lit and when the Mexicans' food and possessions had been burnt, they were branded with a metal rod taken from the flames. George Hanigan took a knife to Bernabe's testicles, but one of his sons restrained him before he cut them off. Finally the ropes were cut and each Mexican, in turn, was told to run back to the border. As they fled, shotgun pellets peppered their bare backs.

The three turned up that night in Agua Prieta's hospital and reported what had happened. Eleazar, the only one not too badly injured to travel, was escorted back to the United States to identify the place where they had been tortured. Shortly afterwards the three Hanigans were arrested and charged with assault with a deadly weapon, kidnapping and armed robbery. From Mexico City several government ministers voiced their opinions, talking of 'racial sadism', while Mexican newspapers commented on the barbarism in Yankee civilisation. In Douglas, where the Chicano majority was then seventy per cent, feelings were polarised between the races. While Anglo sympathies were largely with the Hanigans, some took the view that they would have been better advised to have killed the Mexicans. Torturing them and sending them back to Mexico 'made no sense'.

Sick jokes did the rounds of Douglas's Anglo community: one had it that the Hanigans were holding a Mexican barbecue, to which you were invited to bring your own Mexican. Radio stations in northern Mexico played a song, 'Los Tres Mojados', telling of their ordeal. The prosecution tried without success to get the trial moved outside Cochise County, because of the difficulty of empanelling an impartial jury. Then, a week before the jury was due to be chosen, George Hanigan died of a heart attack. 'Lo castigo Dios' (God punished him) they said in the Mexican American community.

The trial began more than a year after the incident. Almost inevitably, the testimony of the three Mexicans revealed discrepancies; the defence accused them of being burglars; and the defendants declined to give evidence. They were found not guilty on all counts. Tensions ran high on both sides of the border. For a while, Douglas residents were afraid to go shopping in Agua Prieta. The Ku Klux Klan invited its members to patrol the border area, and the Mexican government dispatched troops to Agua Prieta. Tom and Pat Hanigan were advised to leave Douglas until things died down.

But the matter was not allowed to rest with the Hanigans' acquittal. The widespread feeling, not only among the Hispanic community, that justice had not been done reached out of the state of Arizona and as far as Washington. Civil-rights organisations lobbied on Capitol Hill and at the Justice Department. The pressure took time, but two years after the first trial the two brothers were brought before a federal court, charged with violating the Hobbs Act, which prohibits 'interference with commerce by threats of violence'. The three Mexicans were deemed to be commerce since they were on their way to seek employment as farm labourers; the fact that they were in the United States illegally was considered irrelevant. Congressman Sam Hobbs may not have had such a case in mind when he gave his name to this piece of legislation forty years earlier; but a second trial was held, in Tucson, after Manuel, Bernabe (who was now part of a travelling circus) and Eleazar (who had lost his wife and child) had been gathered together, and lasted four weeks. The jury deliberated for six days and failed to reach a verdict. The Justice Department announced a retrial, this time in Phoenix, and in front of two juries, one for each brother. By this time the Hanigans had used up most of their funds in lawyers' fees, and Bernabe was drinking so heavily that he was unable to give evidence. After another month, at the end of which some jurors still failed to grasp the relevance of the Hobbs Act to the plight of the three Mexicans, one all-Anglo jury acquitted one brother and the other all-Anglo jury convicted the other.

Over the next twenty years the immigrant situation in the Douglas area only got worse. The number of arrests in the last decade of the century increased from fifteen thousand a year to two hundred thousand. Two ranchers owning a thirty-mile stretch of border boasted of having caught more than three thousand illegal immigrants in three years, with the aid of tracker dogs and M-16 automatic assault rifles. Locals will tell you that one of the favoured routes used by immigrants takes them across the eastern edge of Douglas, through the town cemetery, where they tramp over George Hanigan's grave.

West of Douglas/Agua Prieta, three Sonora border towns (Naco, Nogales, Sasabe) share names with their Arizona twins, though only

Nogales has a town on the Arizona side of any significance. Naco, Sonora is one of the border crossings known not only for its smuggling of drugs; there is also a good contraband trade in parrots, which are very popular north of the border. The problem is that these birds, trapped by Indians in southern Mexico, may be carriers of the oddly named, and deadly, Exotic Newcastle Disease, which, when it is identified in the USA, usually results in the slaughter of millions of chickens by the Department of Agriculture. The period and cost of quarantine for birds imported from Mexico, and the demand among Americans for parrots and cockatoos, are such that a smuggled bird may be sold for up to a thousand dollars. Pound for pound, I was told, there's more money in parrot smuggling than there is in marijuana. A previous mayor and police chief of Naco were caught in possession of a hundred and sixty contraband birds, which would have doubled their salaries for several years.

The town became more legitimately famous in 1974 when it was visited by President Luis Echeverria in the middle of the night. While the president was dining in Nogales (he was awaiting a border meeting with the newly installed President Gerald Ford), the mayor of Naco addressed him on the subject of his neglected, decaying town which, he said, could only be saved with government help. So impressed was President Echeverria by this eloquent plea – the wine at dinner may have helped both president and mayor towards a sympathetic understanding – that he set off at once by bus to Naco, arriving at 2 o'clock in the morning. (Had he driven instead along the paved Arizona highway from Nogales to Naco, he would have completed the journey in less than half the time.) Having observed, by moonlight, the state of Naco's roads and buildings, and having presumably taken the mayor at his word on the state of the town's schools and the numbers of its unemployed, the president promised on the spot that something would be done. Factories and a community auditorium were built, streets were paved – but the town's revival was short-lived. Nothing much changed, except that the date of the president's visit, 21 October, is marked every year by a day of fiesta. The shoe factory did not last and the asphalt surface of the roads developed potholes which went unfilled. But a few people in Naco grew more prosperous through the increased trade in drugs and parrots.

Outside Naco, not far from the handsome, adobe-style US border station, the international fence has holes big enough to let a vehicle through and in places no more than a single strand of wire. Further west, towards Nogales, the former border post of Lochiel, named by immigrant Scottish cattlemen, is now closed to vehicular traffic, though not, of course, to contraband. This part of southern Arizona so epitomises the old American West that it has been much filmed; it was considered more suitable as the location for the film of *Oklahoma!* than the state in which the story is set.

A pair of walnut trees which once grew in the pass that straddles the border gave their name (in Spanish *nogal* means walnut tree) to the two towns known locally as Ambos Nogales. Nuts are not big business between Mexico and the USA, but vast quantities of vegetables and fruit cross the border here during the winter months. Mexico provides about three quarters of all the fresh produce – tomatoes, onions, garlic, peppers, apples, grapes, melons – eaten in America between October and March, and most of it comes through Ambos Nogales.

Nogales, Arizona was founded as a trading post in 1880 by a Russian Jewish merchant, Jacob Isaacson, who tried giving his name to the town, but it didn't catch on. Nogales seemed somehow more euphonious and more vernacular. But Isaacson did establish an important immigrant tradition: many Jewish familes, also Greeks and Lebanese, came to Nogales and prospered. Cross-border business helped promote good relations between the two Nogales communities, and there was often a fellow feeling between the political refugees from Europe and

❋ DESERT AND THE DEVIL'S ROAD ❋

Nogales: Arizona and Sonora

the economic refugees from elsewhere in Mexico and Latin America. I went to see an elderly Jewish lady, Ruth Epstein, who had lived in the Nogales area all her life and remembered how it used to be.

Her family ran a department store in pre-NAFTA times, when she used to sell bolts of cloth to Mexicans. But the finished goods, made in America, have been widely available south of the border since NAFTA became effective in 1994 – the year in which a major devaluation of the peso also kept Mexicans away from the Arizona shops.

'It has all changed in the past few years,' she said. 'There used to be more communication between the two Nogales. It was not just the commercial contacts – I think we are the only border towns to have built a joint sewage-treatment plant. And we used to cooperate over fire-fighting; but the days are gone when the US Fire Department would hitch up a hose to a hydrant and throw it over the border to put out a Mexican fire. That doesn't happen any more.

'We used to know a lot of families across the line, but now their children have moved away, and so have ours. Nogales, Sonora has become diluted by all the *maquila* workers.'

Mrs Epstein recalls the time when Nogales, Arizona's population was a third of Nogales, Sonora's. Now the Mexican town has 350,000 inhabitants, more than fifteen times more than its American sister. She is not a fan of the *maquiladoras*, which have brought so many more people to the border, more crime and more illegal crossings.

'I used to send my boys over the border for a haircut, without thinking twice about it. But I certainly wouldn't let children go across today – if they weren't robbed they'd be offered drugs.'

Nogales is one of the most popular crossing points for drugs, whether concealed in lorries laden with fruit and vegetables or conveyed underground. Between the hills on either side of the border, tunnels have been dug, connecting to sewer lines and culverts which carry water and debris, including parcels of drugs, into Arizona. Tunnel entrances and exits have been discovered in houses and commercial premises and once, in 1999, in the precincts of the Church of the Sacred Heart in Nogales, Sonora.

The local newspaper, rather grandly called *Nogales International*, was founded in 1925 when the two communities were closer. Today, the editor, Harold Kitching, told me, things were different. His paper did not cover events across the border in Nogales, Sonora 'unless it is something big like a gas explosion' – and he had no correspondents in Mexico. 'I've never met a Mexican journalist I could trust,' was his depressing comment, the more so from a man editing a so-called international newspaper half a mile from the Mexican border. One might have expected the paper to foster a border culture uniting the two towns of the same name, but the reverse appears to be true. It may happen in Tex-Mex country, but not west of the Rio Grande.

Mrs Epstein had hardly a good word to say about present-day Nogales, Sonora, but I found it more colourful, more friendly and cleaner than other Mexican border towns. This, at any rate, was the impression gained close to the border post, where rug stalls, curio shops, Tecate beer signs and shoeshiners abound. Above street level, in both Nogales, the houses and cypress trees standing on the greenish hillsides are almost (but not quite) reminiscent of Tuscany. A few blocks from the border, however, the *colonia* dwellings bear witness to the half-life endured by those (mostly women) who work in the *maquiladoras*. Many of the shacks are made of wooden pallets discarded by their employers and buttressed by walls of tyres taken from abandoned cars. Municipal rubbish dumps nearby are likely to contain dead dogs, their festering corpses clouded by flies in the oppressive heat. Few men are to be seen, having left their women and children and gone to seek work north of the border.

Those with enough pesos cross to Nogales, USA for their provisions. The Safeway and Walmart supermarkets here (known to Mexicans as

Walmarto) have the largest turnover of any of their branches in Arizona. They also come to buy curios from the growing Korean community, who have to suffer the irritation, not to say indignity, of being called *'los chinitos'* by Mexicans. Most of this border junk, as it is less politely known, will be resold in the south after duty, or more likely *mordida* to the customs, has been paid. (In spite of the free-trade principle enshrined in NAFTA, Mexicans may only return from the USA with a limited amount of duty-free goods.) Subject to further devaluations of the peso, wealthier Mexicans find it worth their while to drive as far as Los Angeles to buy goods for resale in their own country; and they will be able to stay more cheaply in a good hotel in Tucson than in a comparable establishment in Hermosillo.

Children cross to Nogales, Arizona to get a free American education, and many Mexicans are in receipt of US welfare cheques via an Arizona post-office box because, though resident in Mexico, they were once registered for employment in the States. You get the impression in Nogales, north and south, that the border is an elastic line which can be pulled and manipulated pretty much at will. Outside the towns it is marked only by barbed-wire cattle fencing, which doesn't keep anyone out. And then comes the desert, where the border line is meaningless, crossed only by Papago Indians and desperate immigrant travellers.

The Papago, now more generally referred to as Tohono O'odham ('Desert People'), inhabit the Sonoran desert. The border bisects their territory but you wouldn't know it. As a ranger put it to me, 'The border has always been somewhat indistinct in this area' – so indistinct that when the line was drawn on a map between Mexico and the United States in 1853, no one thought to tell the Tohono O'odham. But they have maintained ever since that it is not they who cross the border but the border which crosses them. The authorities generally leave the indians alone when they go from one country to the other, but harassment is not unknown. In 1997, the four native American 'nations' with tribal lands straddling the border – Tohono O'odham, Yaqui, Cocopah, Kickapoo – got together to form an Indigenous Alliance Without Borders to bring pressure for their better treatment at international border posts.

Markets are regularly held at cattle fences along the border, where Indians from both sides come to meet and trade. For very good reasons, the great majority of the twenty thousand or so members of the Tohono O'odham tribe live on their reservation west of Tucson, the second largest in the USA. The medical and educational arrangements are a lot better in Arizona than in Mexico; and, most importantly, the Indians have the opportunity to earn large sums of money from the casinos which only they may own and operate in the southern states of the USA. There are some twenty casinos in Arizona; profits from gaming in Tucson in 1999 apparently yielded a dividend of two thousand dollars for every man, woman and child belonging to the Tohono O'odham nation. They also make good money from their woven baskets, which have been known to sell for more than ten thousand dollars each. Farther north, between Navajo and Apache country, the Hopis are noted for their pottery, also for a snake-dance which D.H. Lawrence once witnessed while travelling in these parts in the 1920s. In this ritual, deadly rattlesnakes, revered by Indians as a life-spirit, are held by the dancers in their mouths.

One might suppose that there was little sustenance in the Sonoran desert, whether for Indians or immigrants. In fact this region has been described as one of the most biologically diverse arid areas in the world, and a remarkable variety of flora survives here. Many plants and roots contain nourishment, and the organ pipe cactus is rendered by the Indians into a sweet red jelly. Rare species of antelope (pronghorn) and sheep (bighorn) live in this wilderness. A hog-like animal called the peccary, or javelina, may be shot during a short season (for part of that time only with bow and arrow), but I cannot say whether it makes good eating. Animals and Indians know that water may be found in rock 'tanks', often high up the mountains which rise out of the desert. Information of this sort can be found in booklets such as the one I came across in Tucson – 'How to Survive in a Desert Situation'. But it is not available in Spanish for the benefit of those unfortunate *indocumentados* who, lacking this knowledge, risk death by dehydration as they head north across the desert in summer temperatures well above 100°F.

A priest from northern Italy was probably the first non-Indian to explore the Sonoran desert. Padre Eusebio Kino was born in the Dolomites near Trento in 1645, a hundred years after the council of that city launched the Counter-Reformation. He was a Jesuit missionary, and also a true frontiersman and explorer, initially in Baja California, where he disproved Sir Francis Drake's theory that California (Baja and Alta) was an island. He then mapped much of what is now southern Arizona and northern Sonora, and befriended the Pima Indians, bringing them cattle and teaching them animal husbandry. He spent much of his time in the Pimeria Alta, north of Caborca, where he established a mission in the 1680s and became known as the Apostle of the Pima.

I have seen a composite portrait of Kino, drawn from known data concerning him and his family, which makes him look rather like Clint Eastwood. This intrepid pioneer was one of the first Europeans to follow the Camino del Diablo trail across the desert to Yuma, where he crossed the Colorado River in 1699 and trekked on to the Pacific coast. But he was soon back in the Sonoran desert, in the country which was not then bisected by an international border and which Kino called Pimeria and Papagueria. Santa Cruz, east of Nogales, was one of the towns he founded, and from there he would make his journeys between the two tribal communities, unhindered by any border restrictions. He died in Magdalena, between Nogales and the curiously named (after a revolutionary general) Benjamin Hill, in 1711 while dedicating a mission. I like to think that it may be in honour of the memory of Padre Kino that the Indians continue today to roam at will and ignore the international boundary which was carved through their territory.

The International Sonoran Desert Alliance (ISDA) is one of the more recent relationships which have been forged across the border. It embraces Mexican, American and Native American interests in seeking to 'promote multicultural understanding, communication and education … and community-based economic development, to protect valuable biological resources and guarantee respect for the cultural heritage of the Sonoran Desert'. As a comparatively rare example of cross-border cooperation in this sector, it is unquestionably a good thing. One of the projects inaugurated in 2000 was a joint programme to train schoolchildren in Mexicali to maintain and repair bicycles. US operators of *maquiladoras* in the capital city of Baja California were being encouraged to sponsor environmental programmes in local schools.

The ISDA has its offices in Ajo, Arizona, which I passed through on my way from Phoenix to the border. Despite being no more than a hundred miles south of Phoenix, it took me some time to find anyone who had heard of the town. It is not on the route of any Greyhound bus service, but I eventually found a Mexican company on the outskirts of Phoenix which ran a bus via Ajo to the border and across to the neighbouring Mexican town of Sonoyta. Beyond Gila Bend, where the Gila River bends west towards its meeting with the Colorado River, phallic cacti, the trademarks of the Arizona desert, rise out of the sand and scrub. As we passed through the Barry M. Goldwater Airforce Range (the senator and presidential candidate was born in Phoenix), a USAF jet was circling above the mountains like a buzzard searching for its prey. It would be taking the analogy too far to compare an illegal immigrant to a small rodent in danger of being dive-bombed by the winged predator above, but the training activities of the airforce do constitute an additional hazard for those travelling north to look for work.

I liked the idea of Ajo as A Town Called Garlic, and the origin of its name seemed to be confirmed when I was told that the root of the ajo lily – purple-flowered, which grows locally – tastes of wild garlic. But further enquiries led to a more credible explanation for the town's name: that it was called after the Tohono O'odham word *auho* for the red copper ore which they traditionally use for body paint. Until 1984, when the mine closed, Ajo was a copper town, with one of the world's largest open-pit mines (one and a half miles across), which still lies open today. Refugees from the Mexican Revolution, some of them followers of Pancho Villa, worked in the mine and, fearing they might be pursued as far as Ajo by Mexican government troops, stockpiled weapons in a tunnel beneath a hill overlooking the town. I had read somewhere that a number of Villistas, who stayed on after the war, were buried in Ajo cemetery, but the secretary of the Ajo Historical Society said that no evidence of this was to be found on any headstones in the cemetery. In 1917 much of the town was destroyed by a fire which started with a saloon-bar brawl and Ajo had to be rebuilt. In its centre, two churches face a large, attractive square with palm trees and Spanish adobe-style architecture, seen also in the old railway station which used to serve the copper mine.

Today, the age of copper having come to an end, Ajo advertises itself as the place 'where the summer spends the winter'. It is a refuge for elderly couples from Illinois and Wyoming who can spend the winter months safe in the knowledge that the daytime temperature will seldom fall below 70°F. Seated outside the Deli on the Plaza, in the shade of the white-stuccoed arcade which runs along two sides of the square, the oldies were eating pastrami sandwiches on rye with kosher pickles to remind them of home and drinking iced tea. Several of them took half their lunch home in paper bags. Next door the pharmacy was well patronised by octogenarians stocking up on their medication. Round the corner, the weekly *Ajo Copper News*, founded in 1916, is content to restrict its coverage to uncontentious local affairs. Ajo is only forty miles from the border, but there was scarcely a dark Mexican skin to be seen.

Later that day, I walked uphill towards Ajo's museum, housed in the old St Catherine's Mission, which was founded by Padre Kino in the early years of the eighteenth century. Here I fell in with an elderly winter resident, a retired life insurance agent from Idaho, who pointed out the mine owner's house, built in the 1920s, on top of a hill looking down into the great pit of the mine. Having served for a while as a convent, it had been used until recently as a bed-and-breakfast inn, but was now empty. There were gold and silver tailings in that mine, my new acquaintance said, which might make it worth reopening. When he told me that the old mine owner had married an Indian, I asked him if there was a disapproving tone in his voice. As we watched the wintry sun setting over the hills, he explained that, as a Mormon, his attitude to such matters had changed when Jesus decided that blacks should be admitted to the Mormon Church. Jesus was right about that, we agreed, but I confessed a failure to understand why He apparently condoned polygamous marriage among Mormons.

A few miles south of Ajo, we approached Why. Since I first saw this town marked on a map, its name had intrigued me, even more than that of its neighbour, Garlic. Why, oh why Why? I wondered, imagining there might be some romantic association – as, perhaps, in 'Why do people fall in love?' The answer, I have to report, is prosaic, even bathetic. The town – it is no more than a few modest houses, a service station and a Baptist church – stands at the junction of the roads from Phoenix and Tucson, forming a Y as the two roads join to turn due south towards Mexico. The original idea was to call the town Y, but when its residents learnt that the US Post Office would not issue a zip-code to any town having less than three letters to its name, Y became Why.

Desert and the Devil's Road

After Why we passed through the Organ Pipe Cactus National Monument, named for this unusual species of cactus, and crossed the border at Lukeville, known more familiarly as Gringo Pass. Sonoyta, on the other side, is said to have been visited by Al Capone, giving ostentatious parties here during the Prohibition years, but it is a story which has never been substantiated. US citizens come to Sonoyta today only to take the fast road south, built by US Marines, to the resort of Puerto Penasco (Rocky Point), an hour away on the Gulf of California. I boarded a bus taking Mexicans west on an inferior road, though grandly called Highway 2, through the forbidding Parque Natural del Gran Desierto del Pinacate.

It was 1 December 2000, the day of the inauguration as president of Vicente Fox, a good day to be in Mexico. 'Hoy Cambia Mexico' ('Mexico Changes Today') read a front-page newspaper headline. Everything would now change, he told the people; the bad old days of the party which had ruled the country for more than seventy years were over. At a very insignificant level I found myself wishing that President Fox would do something about the system of military inspections to which our bus was subjected.

Illegal drugs being transported up the coast from the south will cross into the United States either around Nogales or, if they are taken farther west, will be carried along the road on which we were travelling and then probably smuggled into California between San Luis and Mexicali. Young soldiers stop and search all vehicles a mile or so outside Sonoyta and, after nearly three hours driving through empty desert and mountain passes, they are searched again on the outskirts of San Luis. Were both delays really necessary? Was our bus likely to have stopped and picked up a consignment of cocaine in the desert? I heard later that the risk of corruption among the soldiers looking for drugs is so high that after only a few weeks they are dispatched to other duties.

Large quantities of drugs may not often cross the border in these very remote areas, but immigrants do. Between the two military checkpoints, the narrow tarmac road, with no hard shoulder on either side, arrows through the flat, pitiless desert. To the north are the Agua Dulce Mountains of Arizona, their tops catching the sunlight; to the south stretches the Sierra del Pinacate, so desolate that it was used to acclimatise American astronauts to terrain similar to that found on the moon. The cactus was with us for a while, a welcome relief on the otherwise featureless plain, but then it disappeared. Later the road cut a pass through hills almost overhanging Highway 2. We were approaching the truck stop called El Sahuaro which, I had read, is one of the popular starting points for *indocumentados* beginning their perilous walk through the hills and across the desert to US Interstate 8, the road to a better life.

There are several perils which may be encountered by the prospective immigrant here. He may be abandoned by his guide (coyote); threatened, or worse, by drug-smugglers; blown to bits stepping on a hitherto unexploded bomb dropped by the US Airforce in training; or bitten by a rattlesnake. A traveller in the 1930s recorded that 'there was so many rattlers them days that men had to wear stove pipes on their legs to keep them from gettin' bit. And the rattlers strikin' agin' them stove pipes sounded like hail on a tin roof.' But the greatest danger is from the heat and lack of water. Summer temperatures regularly rise above 110°F, often with stifling humidity. John Annerino, a journalist and author who has walked across the Camino del Diablo in August, drank between three and five gallons of water a day. As a Border Patrol officer in Yuma said to me: 'According to medical advice, for a summer journey through the southern Arizona desert you should take so much water with you that you'd need a tanker following behind.' The trek from El Sahuaro to Interstate 8, about sixty miles, would take at least two days, requiring about ten gallons of water for safety. It is, of course, impractical to carry that much. To survive, you have to know the precise location of the few waterholes in the hills, and you have to be fit. Women are less likely to make it, and anyone who has drunk alcohol before starting off is also at a disadvantage.

In his journeys across what he calls America's Killing Ground, Annerino has found a number of skeletal remains of 'John Doe Mexican', often under mesquite trees which provide the only shelter in this merciless wasteland. Sometimes the bodies have had their eyes plucked out by buzzards. A corpse was once discovered hanging by a belt from a mesquite tree. Plastic water bottles are commonly found, some containing urine. One woman was found dead with a supply of diuretics beside her. In 1980, a group of Salvadoran refugees from the civil war in their country were persuaded by coyotes to pay two thousand five hundred dollars each to be led from the Sonoran frontier through the Organ Pipe Cactus National Monument to Gila Bend, a distance of a hundred miles. The Salvadorans were carrying suitcases and little more than a gallon of water each, it was the Fourth of July weekend and it was madness. None of them even made it to the first waterhole at Bates Well; fourteen were rescued in an advanced state of dehydration by Border Patrol trackers and an equal number died. In desperation they had drunk urine and after-shave lotion, they had sprayed deodorant down their throats, and when they died they had dirt and sand in their mouths, having gnawed the ground in the forlorn hope of finding moisture. The same death toll, a group of fourteen abandoned by their coyotes, was reported in the desert near Yuma in May 2001.

Annerino joined a group of four Mexicans walking north from El Sahuaro through the Copper Mountains and across the Mohawk Desert to the Interstate highway. For part of the way they brushed their footprints from the sand, using branches of creosote scrub, in order to elude Border Patrol trackers. It was high summer and they nearly didn't make it, running out of water shortly before they reached the road. There the Mexicans were able to fill their water bottles from an irrigation ditch before heading on north in search of agricultural labour. They had done the trip before; but first-time immigrants are usually escorted by coyotes charging extortionate fees. They are brought by bus from interior Mexico, guided across the desert and, if their coyote has not abandoned them and they reach the Interstate, they may be transported on to Phoenix or Los Angeles. For someone not living in the Third World it is hard enough to think of making this journey once. Yet many Mexicans return to the USA by this route year after year. In the last two decades of the century, José Hernandez, from Chihuahua, made fifteen treks from Agua Prieta across the desert to Willcox, and four five-day journeys from Sonoyta to Gila Bend. Once one of his companions faced an additional hazard and was killed by a bear.

To those who don't survive, usually due to dehydration, tributes are written and sung:

> They left their land,
> a small town in Durango.
> They reached the border
> leaving everything behind.
> But what they were seeking
> was already close by...
> The sun begins to climb
> the heights of the sky.
> The vultures, cawing
> like creatures in the heat,
> swoop to devour
> two men on the ground.
> The heat is infernal
> and a sad wail is heard:
> 'We couldn't make it...
> How I hurt my mother.'

Many immigrants owe their lives to Border Patrol agents who spot them, usually from the air, and rescue them in the nick of time from their dying diet of cactus and urine. They will have failed in their objective, of course, and they will be returned to Mexico; but they will be alive and no less determined to make it next time. Others claim to have been saved by the Lady in Blue, who is said to travel on the winds of God and guide those in trouble to springs of water. She began life as a nun in New Spain in the seventeenth century, and her image was there to give succour to the Forty-Niners, many of them Mexican immigrants, who travelled across the Camino del Diablo to reach the goldfields of California. But hundreds of them failed to find her and perished.

Beyond El Sahuaro we entered the total flatness of the Yuma desert; it was all sand and the hills were barely visible now. We passed another truck stop, La Paloma del Desierto, and occasional fence-posts began to appear, though with no wire attached to them. A few more miles and telegraph poles, with wires, were in evidence, then smoke, a Mexican flag – and another military control point. We were nearing San Luis Rio Colorado and, either side of the great river, cultivation. There were trees bordering the fields, maize, cattle and seagulls.

Between San Luis and Yuma it appears that the river forms the international boundary. The qualification is necessary because, south of Yuma, the Morelos Dam takes the Colorado River into a canal within Mexico. The border in fact runs down the dried-up riverbed or, to be precise, down the line of the deepest river channel. This may change from one year to the next: when floodwaters or melting snow swell the river farther north in Utah, the dam may be opened to let the water flow down its old course. Depending on the volume of water and the rate of flow, the river may alter its course slightly and, when it dries up again, the line of the channel, and hence the border, may have moved. Border Patrol vehicles drive along the riverbed, but there is no border fence or control post. It is not a popular crossing point for immigrants because the large expanse of lettuce and cauliflower fields on the US side (Yuma claims to be the lettuce capital of the world) make concealment difficult. Anyone who gets this far will have had to swim across the fast-moving canal, which claims a number of victims every year.

Outside Yuma the border turns away from the river and makes due west in a straight line for the Pacific Ocean. The Border Patrol's Yuma County sector in fact includes within its area of responsibility a few miles of territory across the Colorado River and into California. As Alfredo Casillas explained to me at the Border Patrol's Yuma County headquarters, there is no problem with crossing state lines because the Border Patrol is a federal organisation. The sector covers about a hundred miles of the international border; along this stretch, during the peak period between March and May, a thousand people are attempting to cross illegally from Mexico into the USA every day. Mr Casillas reckoned they are apprehending about seventy per cent of this number, perhaps half of them in the San Luis area, and the rest in the desert. Over the whole year, in 2000, the Yuma Border Patrol arrested over a hundred thousand immigrants, an average of almost three hundred arrests per day made by fewer than that number of agents. These are remarkable figures: according to the Border Patrol's estimates, which probably overstate their success rate, more than fifty thousand illegal immigrants are getting into Arizona, undetected, every year.

If this figure is reproduced along the entire border, it means that the population of the USA is being swelled each year by around a million *indocumentados* from Mexico and other Latin American countries. Mr Casillas said that in 2000 they had arrested more illegals than ever before. So were there more of them making the journey north, or was the Border Patrol doing a better job of stopping them? Both, he said; there had certainly been more people crossing the border in Yuma County since California's Border Patrol had increased its strength in the San Diego and El Centro areas, forcing immigrants to try their luck farther east where, according to Mr Casillas, the Yuma Patrol was understaffed. Carlos Fuentes has likened the Border Patrol's job to squeezing a balloon: 'What you squeezed here only swelled out over there.'

At least the cocaine smugglers, bringing consignments from Colombia, tended to avoid the Yuma sector; but San Luis was a popular crossing point for the drugs (heroin and marijuana) grown in northern Mexico. We talked about the unfortunate ones who die while crossing this most desolate stretch of the border. The Border Patrol is not, of course, a desert rescue service, but with its fleet of four-by-four vehicles and five helicopters to cover this sector, it is able to save many from a ghastly death by dehydration. As someone of Hispanic blood, Mr Casillas is naturally sympathetic to the plight of immigrants trying to escape Third World misery. His informed opinion is that the majority are not crossing the border merely to look for seasonal 'stoop labour' but are intending to head north for good. He told me of the recent discovery of the bodies of a woman and two children who were attempting to walk the relatively short stretch to the Interstate highway not far from Yuma. The sand dunes here attract young Yumans who race down them on expensive ATVs (all-terrain vehicles), while young Mexicans struggle to walk across the sand with their plastic bags. Thirty-two bodies were recovered in 1999 from the Yuma desert, but the remains of many more would not be found. The true annual figure for deaths from dehydration in that area was probably close to sixty – but no one will ever know. Bodies are sometimes found not far from the oasis of Dateland, beside Interstate 8, which is flanked to the south by tall palm trees visible for miles and providing a landmark for those stumbling desperately towards water.

Trying to put such thoughts aside, I took a look at Yuma's past – violent and adventurous, of course, but less depressing. The early travellers along the Devil's Road (Camino del Diablo) would cross the

Desert and the Devil's Road

Colorado River here on their way west. Indians would take them across in basket-weave boats. When the California Gold Rush started in 1849, however, a ferry was built and a regular service established at what was known as the Yuma Crossing. Then came a military fort and depot, and the Southern Pacific Railroad reached Yuma in 1877. I remembered once seeing a Western called *3.10 to Yuma*, but have no recollection of what part the train played in the film. These days the only passenger train which Yuma can boast is the three-times-weekly Amtrak service between Jacksonville, Florida, and Los Angeles which comes through the town at about 3.10 in the morning. Yuma today is a trim town with some handsome public buildings of the 1920s and, in particular, two fine examples in the art deco style. As I walked along the left bank of the Colorado River, admiring an old Catholic mission on the hill above, a seemingly endless freight train gave a mournful hoot as it clattered slowly over the bridge and into California. My own route would take me south of the border again, but I too was heading west.

Tijuana beach

Chapter Seven

California Dreaming

IN THE first half of the nineteenth century, California was not much affected by what was going on farther south. It was hardly touched by the revolutionary movement against Spain, and the rancher *californios* were virtually autonomous, paying scant attention to government imposed from Mexico City. Upper and Lower California were divided into two provinces in 1804, then united twenty years later, remaining so until Upper California was ceded to the USA in 1848. Admiral Lord Cochrane, fresh from helping to liberate Chile and Peru (he would reappear in the twentieth century as the model for Jack Aubrey in Patrick O'Brian's novels), was chasing Spanish warships off the Lower California coast in 1822, but this barren peninsula was not of great interest to the American pioneers. Before the Mexican–American War, however, several hundred US settlers had begun to occupy northern California, and in 1835 President Andrew Jackson had tried unsuccessfully to buy San Francisco from the Mexican government. America's main concern was that Britain or Russia might have designs on California. The rumour was put about, inspiring an almost paranoid fear in Washington, that Mexico had agreed to hand over California to Queen Victoria in settlement of Mexico's debt to Britain. It was to guard against Russian infiltration down the coast from Alaska that Spain had established a string of missions in the previous century, beginning with San Diego in 1769. America remained worried at the territorial ambitions of the Russian bear and wanted to get its hands on

Upper California as soon as possible. Jumping the gun by two years, a Captain Fremont attempted to make California an independent state in 1846 (he had a bear stamped on his flag), and the US Navy occupied Monterey in advance of the formal handover.

No sooner had Upper California become part of the USA than the gold rush began. By 1849, eighty thousand people had arrived at the coast, by land and sea. Many of those who took the overland route followed the Old Texas Trail, from Galveston via El Paso, Tucson and Yuma. Others came through Mexico by way of Monterrey and Janos or Hermosillo. Whichever road they took, they had to cross the desert trail which came to be known at this time as the Camino del Diablo, for the Devil certainly claimed hundreds of lives desperate to find California gold.

This was truly a pioneering age. A group of Mormons in Iowa and Nebraska raised a battalion in 1846 to join the Mexican War; two thousand miles and six months later, it reached San Diego, where the US flag was already flying. But it remains the longest infantry march in the history of the US Army. Most of the battalion, having been discharged at Los Angeles, went north to Sacramento and participated in the first gold discoveries. The route taken by the Mormon battalion from Santa Fé south-west to Tucson, then following the Gila River to the Colorado River, was used for years after by the stage lines, until the coming of the railways.

Chinese, too, came to California in the mid-nineteenth century, to work in the mines and later to pick cotton and lay track for the new railways. They were the Mexicans of the time, often abused by their employers and denied their legal rights. They lived in poverty and sent most of their earnings back to China. In 1879 a law was passed banning all further Chinese immigration to California. Having supposedly outlived their economic usefulness and been denied US citizenship, many were brutally murdered. So the Chinese went to Mexico instead, where they were also abused and sometimes killed. One of the few places where they could take refuge was Mexicali, which escaped much of the anti-Chinese feeling, not least because for a while Chinese outnumbered Mexicans in the city. There was an Asociación China in Mexicali, two Chinese theatres and even, apparently, a lunatic asylum for Chinese. In the 1920s the city would have been better called Chicali. Prohibition meant good business for the Chinese, who controlled not only the sale of alcohol but also opium dens and brothels. In the city's university museum I found a photograph of an American tourist smoking opium, seated outside the offices of the Compañía Mercantil Chino Mexicana. (Though most of the high-rollers of Hollywood were attracted to the nearer border town of Tijuana, Rudolf Valentino did marry one of his wives in Mexicali.) For the convenience of bootleggers returning to the USA, a tunnel was built under the border, surfacing in Calexico, which later became the authorised pedestrian subway between the two countries. Inevitably, the profits to be made from such trade and the associated vice led to inter-Chinese warfare. Local residents were aware of subterranean shootouts taking place in the tunnels beneath the streets.

Opposition to the Chinese presence in Mexico persuaded many to return to China. They moved on to Macao when the Chinese People's Republic was established and then, at the invitation of President López Mateos in 1958, several hundred came back to Mexico. Mexicali's Chinatown, the Barrio de la Chinesca, having flourished for many years, is today confined to one short street and a few stalls selling clothes. But that street, when I was there, was hung with Chinese lanterns and bells as part of the Christmas decorations. One shop, El Remate de la Chinesca (*remate* means auction or conclusion) seemed to indicate that the *barrio* was coming to an end. But the Chinese influence remains: there is a distinctly Chinese-looking pavilion which stands prominently next to the border fence, and a choice of some sixty

Chinese restaurants in the city. Across the border, Calexico has a Martial Arts Academy, offering courses in kung fu and t'ai chi.

Once the two countries had agreed on the question of responsibility for irrigating the Colorado River valley, the unimaginatively named towns of Mexicali and Calexico were built at the beginning of the twentieth century. American investors harvested melons, vegetables and cotton on both sides of the border, employing Chinese rather than Mexican labour. Later, disputes over water rights between western US states found only one point of agreement: that none of the Colorado's water belonged to Mexico. Mexico retaliated by reminding America that almost all the major tributaries flowing into the lower Rio Grande came from south of the border. If the Valle de Mexicali was going to become parched, so too would the fertile valley of south Texas. President Cárdenas was the man who fought for Baja California's water (a huge statue of him stands on the outskirts of Mexicali); it was he who expropriated the American-owned plantations in the Mexicali valley and who did nothing to disabuse President Roosevelt of his fear that Mexico might once again favour Germany in the world war which was fast approaching. Roosevelt, anxious to ensure that his profession of Good Neighbourliness should have some practical effect, signed a treaty with Mexico in 1944 guaranteeing the flow of Colorado River water to Baja California, providing for dams and international reservoirs on both the Colorado and Rio Grande and setting up an International Boundary and Water Commission.* But no agreement was able to prevent a major escape of saline water from an aquifer upriver in Arizona, nor the boll-weevil infestation which entered Mexico from the USA and put an end to Mexicali's cotton industry, then one of

---

* *In 2002, Mexico was said to have failed for ten years to meet its treaty obligations on the flow of water into the Rio Grande. Drought-stricken Texas farmers were threatening a 'water war'.*

the world's largest. Today the major problem stems from the number of users diverting the Colorado's water further upriver. The fertile Mexican delta which once covered two million acres is now cultivable over less than one-tenth of that area. However, as an earnest of their intent to continue cooperating over the future of the lower river, the USA and Mexico signed a joint declaration in Washington in 2000. It may not achieve much in the short term, but without it Mexicali could be squeezed nearly dry.

Mexicali has been described as 'hooked by tubes like a dialysis patient to the Colorado River'. At a foot below sea level, it is almost unbearably hot in summer. But, unlike other border towns, Mexicali has a purpose unrelated to the border. It is the capital of Baja California: it has its civic pride, it has some pleasant buildings, wide streets and flowering shrubs in the gardens of well-to-do houses, many of which belong to members of the medical profession. (In the city's Yellow Pages directory, I counted sixty pages of *Medico*s. An acquaintance of mine came here from England to be treated, with some success, for chronic asthma.) For a provincial capital, however, one might have expected a central square flanked by public buildings and a cathedral. But Mexicali has no centre: the better hotels and restaurants are at least a mile away from the shabby downtown area, where a distinctly unimposing cathedral stands a few yards from the border fence.

A photograph from the early years of the twentieth century shows a line of trees separating the two towns and marking the international boundary. Today the line is drawn by a fifteen-foot steel fence which divides the pavement along the Avenida Cristobal Colon in Mexico from the back of the Plaza supermarket in the United States a mere ten yards away. Nowhere along the border are the twin towns so close. I watched a Mexican family, parents and a child, in Mexicali talking through the giant steel bars to an elderly Mexican lady, probably a relative, in Calexico. It has been estimated that sixty-five per cent of the wages earned in the *maquiladoras* of Mexicali is spent in Calexico within twenty-four hours. In the Plaza and other supermarkets on the US side of the border, the staff are Mexican, the customers are Mexican, the goods are marked in Spanish, music blares from a Mexican radio station. Only the prices are in US dollars. And yet free passage and intercourse between a Mexican border town and a corner of southern California which has the highest Hispanic population (approaching eighty per cent) of anywhere in the USA are not allowed.

One knows the reasons, of course, but there is unquestionably something grotesque and offensive about these great prison bars, this Tortilla Curtain, dividing Mexican from Mexican. Inevitably the Berlin Wall comes to mind, an impression reinforced as soon as you go through the US border post to Calexico and walk into the International Border Friendship Park, a title which sounds like pre-1989 East German-speak. Apart from myself, the only people in the park were Hispanic. Calexico is so Mexican that in the 1970s Baja California elected a governor who had been born and brought up there. (Another former governor of Baja California, Ernesto Ruffo Appel, who was born in San Diego, was made Border Commissioner in President Fox's government.) From two o'clock every morning about three thousand Mexican workers cross the border, legally, to work in Calexico and on the farms beyond the town in Imperial Valley. But Calexico remains, if not the poorer, then very much the smaller relation, with a population of only three per cent of the state capital's on the other side of the line. Relationships are not as harmonious as they are between adjoining border towns in south Texas. The first English-language Calexico newspaper that I saw accused Mexico, in a front-page article, of causing smog by burning harvested fields too close to the USA.

Knowing of its traditional popularity in Mexico, I had hoped to see a cockfight while in Mexicali. But enquiries soon established that except on special occasions – usually once a year during a town's fiesta –

cockfighting is illegal nowadays. I had missed Mexicali's annual Fiesta del Sol, held in October, when such fights are a feature of the celebrations. Without being privy to information on the clandestine cockfights held on remote ranches, I would have to be content with reading about this macabre sport as it is practised in Mexico. In the 1930s Graham Greene had no trouble finding a cockfight on a Sunday afternoon, as he recorded in *The Lawless Roads*:

> Two cocks were prepared for the ring. Men in big decorated cartwheel hats and tight charro trousers watched behind the fence ... They felt the cocks as if they were buying chickens in the market, plunging their fingers into the feathers; then a procession of horsemen entered, led by a band of fiddlers wearing bright-coloured serapes. They played softly and sang a melancholy chant about flowers ... Two of the charros took little bright spurs out of beautiful red leather cases and bound them on the cocks' feet with scarlet twine, very slowly, very carefully. All this singing and procession was just a prelude to the scurry on the sand, pain in miniature, and death on a very small scale.
>
> ...Three lines were drawn in the sand: death was like tennis. The cocks crowed and the brass band blared from the stone seats and sand blew up across the arena; it was cold in the wind, in the *sombra*, among the hills. And suddenly one felt an impatience with all this mummery, all this fake emphasis on what is only a natural function; we die as we evacuate; why wear big hats and tight trousers and have a band play? That, I think, was the day I began to hate the Mexicans. The cocks' beaks were pressed against each other, and the brass blared, and the cocks were placed on the outside lines, and the band fell suddenly silent. But the cocks didn't fight, death didn't perform; they turned their backs on each other, the spurs giving them an odd stilt-like

walk, and then they stood quiet and indifferent, taking a look around, while the crowd hooted and jeered as if they had been cowardly or unsuccessful bullfighters.

Again their metallic beaks were touched, as if an electric spark could be engendered by contact, and this time it worked. They were released quarrelling in mid-air; it was all over in a minute; there was no doubt of the victor – a great green cock who sailed above the other and forced it down by weight of feathers on to the sand. The plumage blew out like a duster, the thin bird collapsed and flattened, and there was a wicked punch, punch, punch at the eyes. It was a matter of seconds and then the beaten bird was lifted up and held head downward, until blood came out of the beak, pouring in a thin black stream as if out of a funnel. Children stood up on the stone seats and watched it with glee.

Greene does not mention the betting, which is very much a part of cockfighting, but he does say that he attended this fight in a bullring. Bullfighting is, of course, popular throughout Mexico, as it is in all the countries which once formed New Spain. It was recorded in Mexico within seven years of Cortés's arrival. While it is part of Spanish culture and, in Spain, always reported in the arts sections of newspapers, under 'Espectaculos', in Mexico bullfight reports appear in the sports pages – which may indicate the slightly different attitude of Mexicans to what goes on in the ring. My impression is that they look upon bullfights, as upon cockfights, as sporting occasions, to be enjoyed with plenty of noise and colour and excitement, and they have little interest in the finer points of taurine art. It is said that Mexican spectators do not take bullfighting seriously enough, which may be explained by the fact that Mexican matadors tend to be shallow and showy practitioners of their art, or sport. And yet one of the greatest bullfighters of the last century,

Carlos Arruza, who commanded more money for a while than any Spaniard, was born in Mexico.

In most places, as in Mexicali, the bullring is not in the town centre; it may be quite a modern construction, standing near a ring road or a strip of wasteland and looking more like a sports stadium. (Tijuana has two bullrings: a modern one by the sea, standing next to a lighthouse and to the international border, and a smaller ring in the town.) The largest bullring in the world, holding fifty thousand spectators, is in Mexico City and known as La Mexico. Here the *ambiente* was once memorably described by Norman Mailer, paying particular attention to the whores who 'had headdresses and hindquarters not to be seen elsewhere on earth, for their hair rose vertically twelve inches from the head, and their posteriors projected horizontally twelve inches back into that space the rest of the whore had just marched through'. During the main season, between November and March, many of the top-ranking Spanish matadors come to fight in Mexico, but their appearances are limited by a regulation which requires that, at every corrida, two out of the three matadors must be Mexican. The border towns generally hold bullfights during the summer tourist season, with large American audiences, who can also watch bloodless bullfights in California.

Between Mexicali and Tijuana, the brewery town of Tecate used to stage an *encierro*, or running of the bulls through the streets. It was called a Pamplonada, in imitation of the famous annual bull-running in the northern Spanish city of Pamplona, and the idea was to persuade lots of gringos to spend their money in Tecate rather than on the more obvious attractions of Tijuana. The bulls were no more than yearlings; instead of running away from them, the young Americans, full of the local beer, made macho attacks on the unfortunate animals. In subsequent years larger bulls were brought in, and the run came to be more like Pamplona, with a stampede along the Calle Juárez, fenced to stop the bulls escaping down side streets. Then one year a taco stall caught fire, and flames and smoke spread to the main street which the bulls were running down. Because of the fencing, no one could get out and panic ensued, with many being burned and hurt, though the bulls were unharmed. It was all too much for the town of Tecate, and so, after ten pretty chaotic years, the Pamplonada came to en end.

As one of the smaller border towns, Tecate normally presents a gentler face than the two cities on either side of it. When I was there one Sunday morning, I watched families assembling for mass at a modest modern church. An old man approached, wearing a stetson and carrying a crucifix. He appeared to be taking it into church, but as he passed he offered to sell it to me. He had several more in a shoulder bag.

The town is dominated by its brewery; otherwise it has the usual mix of low buildings, Ladies' Bars, dentists, shoeshiners and street sweepers. Few US tourists bother to come here, though it is little more than an hour's drive from San Diego; Tijuana is closer and has much more to offer. In the other direction, Tecate is less than a hundred miles from Mexicali, over a road which twists frighteningly through mountains and sometimes seems about to drop over precipices. Little piles of metal, looking like the remains of vehicles, can be glimpsed far below. West of Tecate, the road falls more gradually, through farmland and olive groves, towards Tijuana and the Pacific Ocean.

I crossed from Tecate to the United States, walking up the steeply inclined street to the border, where a customs officer, looking at my passport, asked what part of England I was from. Hoping to cut short the conversation, I said no more than 'Wiltshire', only to be told: 'Oh, yeah, I went up to Dorset last time I was in London.' My astonishment was such that when, a few hundred yards farther on, I passed Thing Road, the oddity of the name hardly occurred to me. Tecate, USA is marked on some maps, but it consists of little more than a store, a few caravans and the shells of cars abandoned for scrap. No Thing Road would be more appropriate. The border post is closed at night for fear that drug-smugglers might kidnap US Customs agents. (This happened during Prohibition, when the contraband was alcohol.) On the road north-west to San Diego, through groves of oak and sycamore and over brown, boulder-strewn hills, we were constantly seeing Border Patrol vehicles and signs carrying the warning, 'Patrolled by Aircraft'. Crossing a small river called Cottonwood Creek, I saw from the map that it becomes the Tia Juana (Aunt Jane) River south of the border, flowing, when weather permits, through the city which bears its name, then back into the USA where it meets the sea south of San Diego. Thoroughbred horses were grazing well-irrigated fields of lush grass close to the road, which later wound through a mountain pass called Jamul, an Indian word for a weedy place. As we entered California's third city the temperature was about 20°F cooler than at the Tecate border.

The Portuguese explorer Juan Cabrillo made the first landfall here, at Point Loma, in 1542. He called the port San Miguel, but some sixty years later it was given the name of San Diego, after an Andalusian missionary who lived in the fifteenth century. It was not until 1769 that a permanent European settlement was established in San Diego, and the first of twenty-one missions down the coast of Alta California was founded, by a Spanish Franciscan father, Junipero Serra. He is commemorated today by a museum, which stands prominently on top of a hill in the old town, and the mission, San Diego de Alcalá. One morning I sat in the mission garden by a statue of St Francis of Assisi. It is a beautiful and peaceful place, filled with roses and aloes. Many of the worshippers celebrating mass beneath the painted wooden beams of the mission church were elderly Chinese.

San Diego was a popular bullfighting town before the Mexican War of 1846–8; later a reputation for prostitution and gambling in its Gaslamp Quarter came to the ears of the gunfighter Wyatt Earp, who moved here in 1885 after his famous shoot-out at the OK Corral in Tombstone, Arizona. He started three gaming halls in San Diego, and no doubt found its wild hell-raising atmosphere congenial. It was around this time that a local resident wrote: 'It is easy to see that killing Indians is not a very dangerous thing to do in San Diego City.'

Tijuana was the place for a night out for San Diegans in those days; and so it has remained. It boomed during Prohibition, with casinos, bordellos, racetracks – and Hollywood was only three hours way. In El Casino de Agua Caliente, its interiors an outrageous mix of art deco, Moorish, Spanish colonial and Louis XV styles, Clark Gable and Rita Hayworth, Douglas Fairbanks and Jean Harlow danced and gambled many nights away. After the Second World War, they also crossed the border to watch, and bet on, the originally Basque sport of jai alai, or *fronton*, which came to Tijuana in 1947. Caesar's Hotel was responsible for the creation of a salad in 1924, when it was no doubt a grander place than it is today. Now there are no boutiques or kiosks in the hotel lobby, only a pharmacy selling the usual range of cheap medications – and Cuban cigars.

But plenty of tourist boutiques – Ralph Lauren, Tommy Hilfiger – are to be found in the Avenida Revolución. Tijuana is the only border town to have such shops, and to have a hotel belonging to the expensive Camino Real chain. At the tackier end of the tourist trade, there is very little that cannot be bought: wool serapes, leather boots, valium, silver jewellery, styrofoam balls covered with bits of broken mirror and every conceivable sort of trinket sold by Indian women from the south. When you have had enough of being pestered in the numerous arcades along the Avenida Revolución, you can seek refuge with a margarita in a bar where the only intrusion may be the relentlessly repetitive music of a *mariachi* band. Donkeys painted to look like zebras offer themselves at street corners to be photographed with tourists wearing the cliché sombreros. (You never see Mexicans wearing these sombreros; they either wear stetsons or baseball caps.) There is less 'sin-tourism' in TJ these days, you are told. But there are still plenty of disco clubs for Americans to get drunk in, with names like Baby Rock, Ruben Hood and Señor Frog's ; and there is no shortage of prostitutes in the streets of the Zona Norte – they have a union and call themselves Las Magdalenas – and in clubs where US sailors are pleasured by transvestites.

The Zona Rio is in a classier area of town, where shopping is a more dignified experience; and in the Plaza Zapato a truly amazing range of leather goods – from shoes to saddlery – is to be found. One of the more interesting things about Tijuana is its range of people and products from all parts of Mexico. There is no better place to see the variety of the folk art which the country has to offer; and when you get talking to a waiter or taxi driver you may discover that he comes from Oaxaca or Veracruz. Tijuana has a winery and serious bookshops; and it has an impressive Centro Cultural, with one building having the form of an egg (the earth) breaking out of its shell. It also lays claim to being the most visited city in the world. Apparently the border is crossed something like fifty million times every year, if only for a few hours. It is a doubtful honour for a city with the highest level of violence along the border. Some of it is inevitably associated with the huge number of workers from the *maquiladoras* (Tijuana is now the largest television-manufacturing centre in the world) and most of it has to do with drugs (thirty per cent of the cocaine and marijuana sold in the USA passes through the city). It is not unusual, during periods of retribution or the settling of scores, for drugs-related murders to average one a day in Tijuana.

The fate of illegal immigrants is no less shocking. To learn about the situation in the border area which divides the two Californias, I went to see Leticia Jiménez in San Diego, who works for the Border Program of the American Friends Service Committee. Most of the illegal entries, she said, used to take place a little way east of San

Diego/Tijuana, through the canyons of Otay Mesa near the airport. But since the start of Operation Gatekeeper in 1994, the Border Patrol had been making more use of electronic surveillance, had erected fourteen miles of fence and had doubled the number of its agents in the San Diego sector. The annual number of arrests was close to two hundred and fifty thousand, but many immigrants were now trying their luck at more remote border crossings. Beyond Tecate, at Jacume/Jacumba (which Mrs Jiménez warned me not to visit on my own), the hapless *indocumentados* risk being robbed and raped, sometimes by Mexican police, before they reach the USA. When they do so, they may be subject to other human-rights abuses – beatings, assaults, denial of food and water, according to Amnesty International – from Border Patrol agents. Crossings made in the desert and mountains also carry the risk of death from dehydration and hypothermia; others may drown in irrigation canals and in the Pacific Ocean. I was shown a photograph of priests from Tijuana and Los Angeles blessing a group of migrants about to set off on their journey north. In the six years since 1994, five hundred deaths had been recorded in southern California.

On the outskirts of Tijuana, where the city gives way to a mass of flat-roofed shacks, some of them perched on barren, dusty hillsides, a mesh fence runs like a roller-coaster towards the sea. A hundred yards from the beach, the mesh is replaced by corrugated steel sheeting, which projects into the Pacific Ocean. Above the sea, on the Mexican side, stands a lighthouse and, next to it, the Plaza Monumental bullring. On a Sunday afternoon, agents of the US Border Patrol can listen to the *olés* as they sit in their vehicles next to the fence in the Border Field State Park. The bullring makes a bizarre sight so close to the frontier and to the sea. On the other side, there is nothing to see but Border Patrol vehicles cruising up the beach and helicopters flying over the flat, empty land which stretches north towards the high-rises of San Diego. The last bar in Baja California, offering nachos and iced lollies, is called La Michoacana, possibly in tribute to the large number of people from that southern state who take this route to California.

Arturo Mercado Arriaga was one of those Michoacanos who didn't make it. A few yards from the sea a long list of printed names, column after column of them, is attached to the fence. These are, like Arturo, the Migrantes Mexicanos Muertos en la Frontera de California during the past few years. Most of those named were in their twenties, some as young as seventeen. Many were 'no identificado'. Also pinned to the fence is a wreath encircled with barbed wire, holding the meagre belongings of a typical immigrant: a T-shirt, a pair of canvas shoes, a water bottle, a plastic baby doll and an image of the Virgin Mary. At the end of my border journey, this was a moving and melancholy reminder of the hazards of breaking free from the misery of the Third World. Nothing seems to deter the *indocumentados*: a notice warns of 'Corrientes Peligrosas', with an illustration of a man drowning; but men continue to drown trying to reach the US shore by swimming round the end of the fence. On the other side, a party of seagulls stands in the shallows, as if to welcome, or warn, any new arrivals from the sea. Some immigrants get killed crossing the main road between the border and San Diego and farther north on the freeways heading for Los Angeles. 'Caution' signs on these roads depict a distinctly un-Latin American couple running, with the mother pulling her daughter behind her.

Mrs Jiménez reckoned there were, at any one time, something like five million Mexicans living and working illegally in the USA, plus another few million of other nationalities, mostly Central American, who are insensitively categorised as OTMs (Other Than Mexicans). They are ineligible for social security benefits or any workers' compensation scheme. They are able to apply for legal residence after ten years, but it is hardly ever granted. The immigrant must establish that he would face extreme hardship if returned to his own country – something which is almost impossible to prove and which a judge is very reluctant to accept. I asked Mrs Jiménez what she thought of the idea, recently proposed by the lady governor of Arizona, of reviving the *bracero* or guest-worker programme which was established during the Second World War. Permits would be made available for seasonal work, the 'stoop labour' which Americans are reluctant to do, and Mexicans would then presumably be entitled to the benefits which are denied them when they have crossed the border illegally. The US Federal Reserve chairman, Alan Greenspan, had recently said that the only answer to current labour shortages was to increase immigration quotas before the labour market showed signs of inflationary pressure. Mrs Jiménez welcomed that statement, also the surprising announcement that the largest American labour union, AFL–CIO, was seeking an amnesty for undocumented foreign workers. But the memory of the *bracero* programme as it was administered in the 1940s and 1950s was clearly distasteful to her.

'It was often no better than slave labour. I was a child in Tijuana, and I remember seeing queues of Mexicans, each one holding a hat and a *maleta* with their possessions, waiting to be admitted to the USA. First they had to be sprayed – disinfected – by a man wearing a mask. But, and this I can't forget, the poor Mexicans weren't provided with any masks for themselves.

'When the *bracero* programme came to an end, the US government launched Operation Wetback to forcibly "repatriate" Mexicans back to Mexico. But many of them were in fact US citizens.'

More than half a century on, they are still *los de abajo*, the underclass, and the hostility is still there. The culture of confrontation remains, between *mojado* and *migra*, wetback and Border Patrol, between the poor Mexican and the stamp of American authority, between the poor Mexican and the rich, 'liberal', white Californian family so devastatingly portrayed by T. Coraghessan Boyle in his novel *The Tortilla Curtain*. While the border stays closed and manual labour pays ten times more north of the line, the relationship is not going to change. And what about the Mexican–American question? In another novel, *Warday*, an independent Mexican–American country known as Aztlan, with El Paso as its capital, emerges along the border in the aftermath of nuclear war. (In Aztec history, Aztlan is the mythical place, supposedly in Nayarit, from which the people set out on their journey of conquest, finding an eagle perched on a cactus with a serpent in its mouth and so providing Mexico with its emblem and the centrepiece of its national flag.) It may be fanciful to believe in separatist tendencies among the border people, but there is much talk of a border culture, a *mestizaje* (miscegenation) of Mexican and American, as there was of Indian and Spanish, to form a new identity. In some areas the mixture includes native American, Chinese and Korean. There is certainly a sense of community along the border, especially where the Rio Grande forms the boundary, and of shared hardship – there are poor *colonias* in south Texas as well. (In 2001, McAllen declared itself the poorest town in the USA.) The separation of Chicanos, and indeed Mexicans living illegally in the USA, from mainstream American society today is well illustrated by an incident that occurred in a Texan town just south of El Paso in the late nineteenth century. An Anglo entrepreneur had tried to stake a claim outside San Elizario to salt deposits which the local people, on both sides of the border, had worked jointly as common property on the basis of grants made by the Spanish government. There was an uprising, and at the end of the affair the Anglo lost his claim and none of the rebels was punished. Mexicans from the Chihuahuan riverbank took part in the disturbance and gave sanctuary to the *tejanos*. A board of investigation commented, in its report, that:

> The inhabitants of the adjacent towns on both sides of the river ... are intimately connected by the bonds of a common faith,

like sympathies and tastes, and are related in numerous instances by marriage ... The people on the left bank of the river were supposed to be American citizens and their cousins a hundred feet away on the other side of a sometimes nonexistent stream were supposed to be Mexicans. Most of them paid no attention. They and their ancestors had passed and repassed the river at their pleasure for ten generations, and the idea of a 'boundary', set up by a handful of gringos who had moved in only twenty-five years before, was a little comic.

But it was not comic for the hundred thousand or so Mexicans affected by the boundary changes in 1848 who had all become, willy-nilly, citizens of the United States to find they would for generations suffer repression and discrimination at the hands of their adopted country's 'white' citizens. Chicanos recall the famous saying of their hero Benito Juárez: 'Among men as well as among nations, respect for others' rights is peace.'

The bonds with the old country remain, of course, as much for old Chicano families as for more recent immigrants. But this is not to say that today's Chicanos look longingly south. In the words of Professor Oscar Martínez, sometime director of the Center for Inter-American and Border Studies, 'For them the border has come to represent a line that separates progress from backwardness, order from chaos, lawfulness from lawlessness, honesty from corruption, and democracy from domination by a privileged few.' This is also true, to an extent, of the *fronterizos* and *norteños* (people of northern Mexico, living close to the border), who have long been considered a special breed by other Mexicans because of their comparative isolation from the rest of the republic. In the Mexican border towns, everything can be paid for in US dollars. 'So far from Mexico City, so close to the United States' might be said of the *fronterizos*, adapting the traditional saying, though for most of them it is seen as an advantage. Many are wannabe Chicanos, with relatives living on the other side who will become more a part of the American mainstream as the Hispanic proportion of the US population increases.

Fronterizos have long been criticised for allowing themselves to be 'demexicanised', for adopting American customs and habits, and a border language whose colloquialisms and grammatical construction may be incomprehensible to Spanish speakers in other parts of, say, Chihuahua and Texas. It is part of the *mestizaje*, which is found too in the border cooking, combining both Mexican and American tastes (the worst of both, some would say), and in the macho enthusiasm of Americans for taking part in contests to eat the most jalapeño chiles (a fiery sort from Jalapa, near Veracruz). But none of that makes the border country a third country, as it has been called. It is a third country only in the limited sense that both *fronterizos* and Chicanos are, to a degree, detached from their own countries, living in a border zone which they sometimes like to call Amexica. There is, as one American academic has put it, 'a concept of overlapping territoriality [that] reflects the functional interrelationship which exists along both sides of the binational border'. That the border area has a high level of violence associated with the drugs trade, with the number of Mexicans who have migrated from the south to work in the *maquiladoras* and with the flow of illegal immigrants to the USA is simply a depressing fact of border life. Nor is the relationship between Mexican and Mexican American necessarily always one of harmony and shared aspirations. In some respects they are not united by common ancestry or by American influence but, adapting the words of George Bernard Shaw on England and America, are divided by a common language. A more liberal immigration policy, under discussion between Presidents Bush and Fox, would not be welcomed by Chicanos whose jobs might be under threat from Mexicans prepared to accept lower wages. On the other hand, Mexicans may be resentful of those who went north and assumed a *pocho* (literally pale-face, i.e. culturally corrupted) lifestyle, becoming American, diluting their language with Americanisms and sometimes their Latin blood too. Attitudes and assumptions may alter as the status of the border changes, but the need to contain immigration, drug-smuggling and now terrorism will militate against a more open border for some time to come.

Chapter Eight

Mexican Habits Die Hard

PAST EL PASO airport and the Fort Bliss military reservation, then up the Transmountain Road, I found a museum dedicated to the work of the Border Patrol. It tells the seventy-five-year history of the organisation, in photographs and a video film, together with a range of exhibits. There is a smugglers' boat, ingeniously made from the bonnets of two lorries. Beside an OH6 helicopter, a notice informs visitors that 'its duties only involve Search and Rescue. BP aircraft have no guns' – which may give some scant comfort to illegal immigrants as they cower in the Texas mesquite. Those BP agents killed in the line of duty (three of them in 1998, including the first woman officer to die on the border) are commemorated by name, also with paintings and a poem. But the most conspicuous memorial is to Rocky, an Alsatian dog who, between 1987 and 1994, helped in the seizure of $75 million of drugs, an achievement meriting a mention in the *Guinness Book of Records*. A white porcelain bowl, known as 'Rocky's Urn', holds the dog's ashes and is displayed behind glass, beside his own Border Patrol green jacket. Rocky clearly did a great job over the seven years of his working life. But with about a hundred tons of cocaine coming into the United States through the El Paso sector every year, he was not able to make much impression on this frighteningly big business.

Smuggling has, of course, been endemic for generations along the American–Mexican border; and in many families the occupation of *contrabandista* has a long and, some would argue, not dishonourable tradition. Firearms came south during and after the revolutionary years, alcohol went north during Prohibition, refrigerators have been crossing into Mexico ever since they were invented. The trade in drugs originating in Mexico and destined for the United States received a temporary setback in the 1970s after a crop-eradication programme run jointly by the Mexican army and the Nixon administration. So the centre of production moved to Colombia and Mexico became instead one of the prime conduits. When a major distribution network, by means of Cessna aircraft through Florida, was broken up in the 1980s, Mexico became the route for eighty per cent of the cocaine entering the USA. Together with Colombia, Bolivia and Panama, Mexico became one of Latin America's most important 'narco-democracies' – still manufacturing heroin and marijuana from its own plantations as well as channelling cocaine from Colombia.

Mexico has had its social revolution, which persisted bloodily for some years, and in spite of economic misery, peso devaluations, huge wealth concentrated among a few and widespread poverty and illiteracy among the majority, it is unlikely to have another. Instead of mob rule, however, the country has been taken over by drug mafias or cartels. They control billions of dollars, a large proportion of them used to influence almost every arm of government, including the highest politicians in the country. During the 1990s, the director of the US Drug Enforcement Administration said he couldn't fully trust any Mexican law-enforcement agency.

In Mexico it is the federal judicial police (*federales*) who are responsible for combating the drugs trade and who report to the attorney-general. When corruption begins in the attorney-general's office, it is not so surprising that about thirty per cent of *federales* were sacked during the 1990s for being on the drug cartels' payrolls. The commander of the *federales* in Matamoros was caught with five million dollars in his office, given him by Juan Garcia Abrego, head of the Gulf cartel.

❧ Mexican Habits Die Hard ❧

Illustration from *La calavera de Cupido*
by José Guadalupe Posada

Garcia Abrego had taken over a smaller and less lucrative smuggling business from his uncle and then expanded into drugs, controlling the border from Juárez to Matamoros and the Gulf Coast round to the Yucatán peninsula. Mario Ruiz Massieu was not the first deputy attorney-general who vastly enriched himself thanks to Garcia Abrego and the two other major cartels, based in Tijuana and Juárez. Regular payments to him and other politicians of a million dollars a month were not exceptional; they help to explain the adage that a Mexican politician who is poor is a poor politician. Ruiz Massieu was later indicted in the USA on drug-trafficking and money-laundering charges, and in September 1999 he took his life. In a suicide note, he blamed the then president, Ernesto Zedillo, for his and his brother's deaths, which seemed a bit unfair. Six years previously, Ruiz Massieu's brother, José Francisco (Pepe), who was general secretary of the ruling Partido Revolucionario Institucional (PRI), had been murdered. The former president's brother, Raul Salinas, was eventually (in 1999) held responsible and sentenced to a jail term of fifty years, reduced to twenty-seven on appeal.

The unravelling of all the threads linking the drug barons and the Salinas and Massieu families would be an almost endless exercise. What can be simply stated is that Raul Salinas had something like a hundred and fifty million dollars in various foreign bank accounts, in Switzerland, London and France, and that this was unquestionably drugs money. (One of the charges against him referred to 'inexplicable enrichment'.) His sister, Adriana, was formerly married to Pepe Ruiz Massieu, which makes the murder, supposedly by his brother-in-law, all the more intriguing. Two other murders took place at about the same time – of Cardinal Posadas (which allegedly involved the Tijuana drugs cartel) and of Luis Donaldo Colosio, who was the PRI candidate chosen by Carlos Salinas to succeed him as president in 1994. The extent of Salinas's direct involvement in all, or any, of this may never be precisely established. Certainly he and his elder brother Raul were very close (it would be another six years before he publicly disowned him). But Salinas's decision to exile himself to Ireland after his presidency ended indicated at least his concern that he might face charges of complicity in drug trafficking, if not murder.

The problem with Colosio was that he had promised to clean up the workings of government and tackle the drug cartels, with which he was probably involved. Before Carlos Salinas left the country, he was apparently so distressed at allegations that he was implicated in Colosio's death and responsible for the recent peso devaluation crisis that he decided to protest his innocence by fasting. It was pure coincidence, he said, that on the same day in February 1995 that he began his fast, his brother was arrested. While Carlos Salinas may never be tried for offences relating to drugs or the murder of his associates, he had no intention, during his term of office, of reforming the narco-democracy over which he presided. He also, by means not exactly in the public interest, enabled a number of rich businessmen, most of them his friends, to become considerably richer.

According to Henry Kissinger, Salinas's achievement was to have 'fostered economic liberalisation that gave freer play to competitive forces and tempered the state's domination of the economy'. But it was mainly in order to pay off foreign debt that Salinas privatised some three hundred state-sector companies. Since their purchasers were often persuaded to pay the government a lot more than their book value, some compensation had to be offered. For instance, shortly after its privatisation the Telmex telephone company, headed by Carlos Slim, was authorised by the president to increase the costs of its service by some two hundred per cent. There was no corresponding improvement in the quality of the service, and Salinas assured Slim that his company's monopoly would be safe from foreign competition for at least ten years. (Slim, the son of a Lebanese merchant, made his first fortune in real estate and tobacco. He was known as Salinas's bagman, fronting for the president's profitable investments in land and other enterprises. He later acquired a substantial stake in Televisa, which was notoriously uncritical of the government, and concluded a deal with Bill Gates's Microsoft computers.)

Protective measures for Mexico's newly privatised businesses were not jettisoned in Salinas's other great achievement for his country, his paymasters and his friends – the North American Free Trade Agreement (NAFTA), signed in the last year of his presidency. The 'Mexico Twelve', as the biggest billionaires came to be known, had time to protect themselves from foreign competition before trade became too tiresomely free. Salinas spent huge sums lobbying for the agreement in the United States, both in Congress and among the Mexican-American community. He wanted to encourage more US investment, and he was able to convince President Clinton that a strong Mexican economy would assist the development of democracy in the country. But the political system remained backward and corrupt, and Mexico was still at best an 'authoritarian democracy', in which, as the author Carlos Fuentes has said, the word 'accountability' has no meaning, indeed is not translatable into Spanish. (*Responsabilidad* does not really cover it.) The free-market economy and free trade with North America are all very well, but they do not exclude freer and more lucrative trade in cocaine. In the first four years of NAFTA, the number of border arrests involving the seizure of drugs increased by more than seven hundred per cent.

In pursuing his free-market and more ostensibly democratic philosophy, President Salinas thought it was time for the PRI, which had been the government party for more than six decades, to be seen to distance itself somewhat from the executive. The party should raise its own funds in future rather than get them from the government. The drug cartels would, of course, make their own contributions to the official party, to the status quo, but the legitimate private sector should also be approached.

Mexican Habits Die Hard

And so a dinner party came to be given, on 23 February 1993, attended by thirty of the wealthiest businessmen in Mexico. It was intended as a private dinner, but this Billionaires' Banquet, as it was dubbed, was to become notorious and a public embarrassment to the presidency.

It took place in the wealthy Polanco neighbourhood, in the house of a former finance minister. No Mexican dishes were on the menu that night; you could hardly offer Château Latour with stuffed chiles. According to one account, the guests were given smoked salmon, steak au poivre and vanilla ice cream with hot chocolate sauce. President Salinas sat at a small table with his host and the PRI president. The businessmen sitting at the large, U-shaped table included Roberto Hernandez, the Banamex banking tycoon; Emilio ('El Tigre') Azcarraga, who as head of Televisa was doing all he could to perpetuate the rule of the PRI, described by Mario Vargas Llosa as 'a perfect dictatorship'; Carlos Hank Gonzalez, who belonged to a vastly rich family and was said to have links with the drug cartels and to control a rent-boy network in Mexico City; and Carlos Slim, who, after Azcarraga's death, would succeed him, according to *Forbes* magazine, as the richest man in Latin America. They all knew they would be asked to dig fairly deep into their pockets to fund the 1994 election campaign. But the size of the suggested contribution came as a bit of a shock to some of those present; by the end of the evening the average sum committed by each guest was twenty-five million dollars. It added up to a staggering total: Mexico's gross domestic product represented about five per cent of the GDP of the United States, yet it had raised in contributions more than five times the amount spent by the Democrats in the 1992 US presidential election. Little wonder that this caused a political scandal in a country where the gap between rich and poor was growing ever wider – and where there were more private jets than in any other Third World country.

Eighteen months later, Ernesto Zedillo was elected president, and the calamitous peso devaluation came three weeks after Salinas had formally handed over to his successor. It was the perfect example of the phenomenon known as *la crisis sexenal*, the economic recession which recurs every six years at the time of the presidential handover. Outgoing presidents have been notoriously successful in postponing or concealing a financial crisis until they have left office. Though the peso was overvalued by about thirty per cent towards the end of Salinas's term, he later tried to hold his successor responsible for the flight of capital through having allegedly warned Mexican businessmen of the imminent devaluation.

Thanks to economic growth and strong reserves, Zedillo was able to avoid another *crisis sexenal* when he stood down at the end of 2000. During his term he allowed a bit more democracy into the system – for the first time the ruling party (PRI) lost control of the Chamber of Deputies and of Mexico City – but he did not initiate major political reform. He brought in one small but significant change, however, within three months of taking office, by breaking with the tradition of immunity from prosecution for ex-presidents and their families. When Zedillo authorised the arrest of Raul Salinas, a gun battle between the federal judicial police who went to his house and Salinas's own armed guards was only narrowly averted. The following month, bodyguards looking after the president's son had to intervene to prevent the boy being mugged by police agents.

If anything, the culture of violence and corruption, usually associated with drugs, seemed to worsen during the 1990s. Following the murder of the presidential candidate Luis Donaldo Colosio and the activities of the brothers Salinas and of Ruiz Massieu, the arrest in 1997, on charges of aiding drug traffickers, of the man appointed to direct the war against the drugs trade in Mexico was acutely embarrassing. (But it was such a good story that it resurfaced three years later in a film, *Traffic*, starring Michael Douglas. That part of the story which takes place in Tijuana had to be filmed in Nogales, Sonora after the film company received death threats from the Arellano Felix drugs cartel.) General Jesus Gutierrez Rebollo was head of the National Institute to Combat Drugs and had been praised by his counterpart in the US Drug Enforcement Administration (DEA) as a man of 'absolute, unquestioned integrity'. A few weeks before his arrest, the general was in Washington getting the latest US intelligence on Mexican drug-traffickers. For the previous seven years, however, Gutierrez had been protecting and passing information to perhaps the most powerful of all the drug-traffickers: Amado Carrillo Fuentes, head of the Juárez drugs cartel. When Mexico's defence secretary heard that Gutierrez had acquired a property with a value far beyond the reach of his salary, he called him in for questioning. The interrogation led to the sixty-two-year-old general suffering a heart attack prior to being arrested and charged with having assisted the Juárez cartel in transporting cocaine across the US border in exchange for property, vehicles and cash.

The arrest was announced on 18 February 1997. Within days the *New York Times* had accused two Mexican state governors of being implicated in the drugs traffic, and similar allegations were publicly made against Raul Salinas and his father. In the same week President Clinton was due to sign the annual certification, under the Foreign Assistance Act, that Mexico was continuing to cooperate in efforts to stop the export of drugs to the United States and therefore should once again receive aid from Washington. Despite compelling evidence to the contrary, and some talk on Capitol Hill of a qualified decertification, Clinton signed as usual rather than risk upsetting the highly sensitive relationship between Mexico and the USA. On the day that certification was given, the brother of Juan Garcia Abrego, former head of the Gulf drugs cartel (and serving eleven life sentences in the USA), inexplicably walked out of the Mexican jail where, while doing time for laundering drugs money, he was reportedly enjoying hotel comforts, which included cable television and the use of a telephone.

❧ Mexican Habits Die Hard ❦

President Clinton sent his DEA head to Mexico, then went himself, to stiffen Zedillo's resolve to combat the escalating drugs trade and the associated corruption in high places. Later the same year, he substantially increased the Justice Department's budget for the border, providing for more Border Patrol agents, and more agents of the DEA and FBI, to police the two-thousand-mile stretch of mostly desolate country between the Pacific Ocean and the Gulf of Mexico. But it was to little avail. Illegal immigrants say, 'Dios es mas grande que la migra' – 'God is more powerful than the Border Patrol.' So is the drugs traffic.

Worrying as the drug problem was to Clinton, most of his public utterances on the subject concentrated on Colombia rather than Mexico. The Mexican and US governments were on excellent terms; Colombia was the problem. Until it was signed in 1993, NAFTA was the predominant issue between Mexico and the USA. On the day that Colosio, the presidential candidate, was assassinated – it was almost certainly a drugs-related murder – Clinton made a statement reassuring Mexico that the NAFTA negotiations remained 'in good shape'.

Once the free-trade arrangements were in place, the US administration continued throughout the 1990s to view trade relations with its southern neighbour, and the maintenance of a strong Mexican economy, as all-important. President Clinton told the Mexican people in 1995: 'The stronger our trade, the greater the well-being of all our people, the better we will be able to fight together our common problems like drugs and crime and pollution.' But he neglected to insist on any greater cooperation between the two countries over the drugs issue when NAFTA was signed. Both countries convinced each other, and themselves, that Mexico's greater prosperity would be good for the development of a democracy freed from authoritarianism, corruption and drugs trafficking. Certainly the balance of trade since NAFTA came into operation has been substantially in Mexico's favour, through its exporting of manufactured goods, fruit and vegetables, foreign cars and television sets. But legitimate trade is inevitably entangled with the drugs traffic; so many Mexican businesses are also secretly involved in the drugs trade, for instance through laundering drugs money. A DEA official was quoted as saying: 'You sometimes have US embassy personnel in Mexico negotiating trade deals with a person who is also facilitating major drug-trafficking into the USA.' And so, buoyed by NAFTA, the export of drugs flourished and increased up the 'narco superhighway' to the USA, prompting one US ambassador to call Mexico the world headquarters of drug-trafficking. Drug use by Mexicans also increased, particularly in the border towns where drug-taking by children was said to be three times the national average.

Colosio promised greater democracy for Mexico in 1994 and probably got killed for it. Six years later, the PRI's candidate for president, Francisco Labastida, invoked Colosio's memory to promise social justice and more honest government, while on the US border the drug cartels decided it was time to remind the government of the real source of power in the country. Carrillo Fuentes, known as 'Lord of the Skies' for the number of large aircraft he used for transporting cocaine from Colombia, had died following plastic surgery n 1997, and shortly after General Gutierrez Rebollo's arrest for being on the drug baron's payroll. The influence of the Juárez cartel suffered no more than a temporary setback; it was the Tijuana cartel, however, run for years by the four Arellano Felix brothers, which excelled itself in brutality in 2000. (As well as being a conduit for cocaine, Mexico produces significant quantities of the heroin, marijuana and mephamphetamines which are smuggled through Tijuana. Mexican heroin is grown predominantly in the impoverished states of Oaxaca and Guerrero, then processed farther north in Sinaloa.) During the first three months of the year, the figure for murders or 'executions' by drugs gangs in Tijuana amounted to about one a day. President Zedillo, on a visit to Baja California at the end of February, promised a crackdown and a review of the efforts of the federal authorities, who were suspected of complicity with the Arellano Felix cartel, to contain the violence. 'We have to make these criminals understand ... that the only homes they deserve are the prisons,' the president said. Two days later, the Tijuana police chief was driving home after Sunday mass when he was ambushed by gunmen in cars and died in a hail of bullets. It was a killing reminiscent of 1920s Chicago, as was the murder, in the same month, of the police chief of the border town of Reynosa, who was shot dead in a restaurant frequented by tourists.

The *plata o plomo* (silver or lead) option had been offered to three government agents who declined the silver and were given the bullet in the spring of 2000. Their bodies were dumped in a ravine outside Tijuana; one of them, a senior federal prosecutor, had had most of his bones broken and his back was imprinted with a vehicle's tyre marks. Another police chief was killed in the state of Sinaloa where Labastida, when he was governor, had apparently been threatened so frighteningly by the Arellano Felix gang that shortly afterwards he left the country to become ambassador in Portugal. Perhaps because it was a presidential election year, the law-enforcement authorities did arrest two senior members of the Tijuana cartel and two Mexican army generals in their sixties who were charged with aiding drug-smugglers; but it was little more than a token gesture.

There was hope that the new president, Vicente Fox, would reverse what he described as his predecessors' policy of 'brushing the narco problem under the carpet'. He established a new organised-crime unit with American assistance, and the Mexican Supreme Court, no doubt emboldened by Fox's public declarations of intent, ruled that drug suspects could in future be extradited to the USA for trial. But the problem was brought once again to public attention early in 2001 when the head of the Sinaloa cartel, Joaquin 'El Chapo' Guzman, escaped from a high-security prison near Guadalajara, evidently with inside assistance. The new president demanded action, and more than seventy prison guards and officials were arrested. The following month a museum was opened in the offices of the defence secretary in Mexico City, exhibiting among other trophies Guzman's gold-handled pistol, encrusted with emeralds and zircons. There were photographs of *quesadillas*, doughnuts, sandals, a pile of telephone directories, an ambulance – all of them had been found stuffed with drugs – and of a woman with heroin-filled buttock implants. In 2002, the president ordered the closure, by bulldozer, of Tijuana's notoriously lawless La Mesa gaol, which was almost indistinguishable from one of the city's red-light districts. Mexico's endemic corruption and criminality were not going to be ended in the six years of Fox's presidency, but he was doing his best to make a start.

From an aircraft arriving in Mexico City, the overpopulation and poverty can be guessed at merely by looking down on the vast blanket of flat-roofed, grey, rough-cast tenement blocks and rectangular shacks squatting cheek by jowl almost as far, even at five thousand feet, as the eye can see. Most of the hillsides are covered not with trees or scrub or parched grass but with the dirty pinks and mauves and blue-greens of thousands of hovels, which look not brighter but more miserable for their ugly colour-washes. More than twenty million people are laid out below on this smudged canvas; sixty years ago the capital city's population was one million. In its centre the residents of some wretched *colonia* were trudging round the huge Plaza de la Constitución (the Zócalo) with placards demanding 'Agua y Drenaje'. Some carried small children and held umbrellas to protect them from the burning sun; others carried red and white flags of indeterminate significance. None of them looked as if they expected their demands for water and drainage to be met. They responded to the megaphoned shouts of a woman in a van – sounding from a distance like an authoritarian call to work or to arms – with a muted, defeatist chorus.

❖ Mexican Habits Die Hard ❖

The box dwellings of the poorest districts of Mexico City are depressing enough, but so too are the habitations of the marginally better off. While looking down from the top of the Pyramid of the Sun at Teotihuacan, I observed the symmetry, the squares and right angles of the ancient Aztec city, and began to understand the modern Mexican's love of this building form. On the road north from Mexico City we passed row upon row of identical, bright orange, concrete cartons. These were not slum dwellings – many of them had cars parked outside – but they stood huddled together within a concrete and wire enclosure, without even a patch of grass between them. Here, it seemed, was the Aztec legacy adapted to modern living in an authoritarian state. The library of the University of Mexico looks back more obviously to Aztec tradition, with its richly figured, polychromatic, rectangular exterior walls, but its box-like appearance is reminiscent as much of Stalinist eastern Europe as of ancient Mexican–Indian civilisation.

While Aztec remains are to be seen a few yards from the Zócalo, the predominant architectural impression in the city's centre is still Spanish, no building more so than the cathedral which, in Graham Greene's words, 'sails like an old rambling Spanish galleon'. However, there is something unmistakably Mexican about the twin towers above the baroque façade: the tower on the right, as you face the cathedral, is a few feet taller than the left-hand one. Over the centuries, and with a little help from earthquakes, the cathedral has settled into its soft foundations.

After the destruction of the Indian religion by the Christian conquistadores, it is fascinating to find these two great shrines (the remains of the Aztec Templo Mayor and the Spanish cathedral) almost side by side. At the junction of the city's two main arteries, the Paseo de la Reforma (laid out by Emperor Maximilian) and the Avenida Insurgentes, the torture and execution of the last emperor of the Aztecs, Cuauhtemoc, at the hands of the Spanish are graphically depicted on the pedestal of his statue. Columbus, not Cortés, is commemorated here, for having brought the Catholic faith to Mexico, though Cortés was rather more of an evangelist than the discoverer of the New World. One reflects on the unquenchable enthusiasm, shared by Spaniards and Indians, for murder and mutilation in seeking to satisfy their respective gods, and on the mingling of Spanish and Indian blood which produced a people so casually indifferent to violent death.

The savage imagery of Diego Rivera's murals is appropriately displayed in the Palacio Nacional, where so many Spanish viceroys and Mexican presidents have bloodthirstily held sway over their subjects. (The remains of two murdered presidents are said to lie in a monumental arch elsewhere in the city.) In the streets around the Zócalo I kept seeing posters for an exhibition of *instrumentos de tortura* at the Palacio de la Inquisición. Modern methods of torture are practised principally by drug gangs unhappy with those law officers who decline to do their bidding.

D. H. Lawrence, who travelled in Mexico in the 1920s, wrote of Mexico City that it 'doesn't feel right – feels like a criminal plotting his next rather mean crime'. (He went on to be rude about Mexican socialists and to make the somewhat politically incorrect comment that seventy per cent of the population were 'real savages, quite as much as they were three hundred years ago'.)

Before arriving in Mexico City, I was warned more than once not to walk in the streets unescorted, and not to wear a watch or signet ring. If you carry credit cards, I was told, and you are mugged, you may be frogmarched to the nearest cash machine and told to withdraw the maximum sum. An inability to remember your pin number under pressure might or might not be genuine, but it would not be treated sympathetically. Finding one cash machine flanked by two armed guards, I was not entirely sure whether they were there for the customer's protection or to ransom him at gunpoint.

In Mexico, uniformed officers cannot always be trusted to act in the public interest. The police are notoriously badly paid: they may not rob banks, but almost all of them are corrupt. *Mordidas*, whether paid to traffic police or to customs officers at the border posts, are part of Mexican life; but it is not always a harmless practice. A woman journalist in the city told me she would never forget the day her mother was driving her to see her dying father in hospital. They were stopped for a minor infringement, and when the policeman learnt how desperate they were to get to the hospital, he demanded that the mother hand over her necklace and watch before allowing them to go on. The last mayor of Mexico City, Cuauhtemoc Cárdenas, claimed to have reduced the crime rate and arrested about two thousand police officers and federal judicial agents. The majority of killings have a Mexican character – because they are prompted by the cult of machismo, or they are the work of *pistoleros* or police agents – and will always remain commonplace. And the rest of the 'mean crime' to which Lawrence referred is as endemic as ever. But this is not to say, with Lawrence, that the city doesn't feel right. It feels right because it feels Mexican, and nowhere more typically than in the Zócalo, by day and night.

The Zócalo is the second largest square in the world (only Red Square in Moscow is larger). Plenty of police are in evidence: public security police and auxiliary police, armed with weapons and plastic shields and, more importantly, their lunch-boxes, which they often carry in their upturned helmets. I walked over to the Palacio Nacional, to be confronted at the entrance by about twenty military police, some of them sitting on benches. Demands for identification were dropped at once when I said I hadn't any, and I went in to admire the Rivera murals. From the courtyard I could see a soldier canoodling with his girlfriend in the palace gardens. It is from the balcony of the palace that the president, every year on the night of 15 September, calls the *Grito de Dolores* – the battle-cry uttered by the priest Miguel Hidalgo in 1810 which signalled the start of the revolt against Spanish rule. The

❧ Mexican Habits Die Hard ❧

Independence Day celebrations begin with the president's *grito*, and the cry is taken up by thousands in the square below.

When I was there in February, I became fascinated, and not a little confused, by the national flag ceremonies taking place every day in the middle of the Zócalo. Staying in the old Hotel Majestic in a room which overlooked the square, I was woken the first morning before six a.m. by the sound of bugles and drums and, in my semi-conscious state, wondered for a moment if I was hearing Santa Anna's call for the final storming of the Alamo. Buglers and drummers accompanied the huge furled flag, carried by eleven soldiers, from the palace to the flagpole. The great green, white and red symbol of the Estados Unidos Mexicanos, with the national emblem of an eagle on a cactus devouring a snake against the white background, was raised to a roll of drums. At sunset the ceremony was repeated in reverse. For most of the afternoon war-dancing Indians in feathered head-dresses had been jumping up and down in the Zócalo – a form of Aztec aerobics? – to the constant thud of drums. They paused for a few minutes while the presidential drums took over for the business of returning the flag to the palace, then went on thumping and jumping into the evening. I left the hotel for an hour or so, and by the time I got back to the Zócalo was amazed to see the flag up there again, billowing overhead. Perhaps the Mexican military take the view that once the traditional lowering of the flag at sunset has been completed, a bare flagpole is a poor thing to look at all evening in the middle of the square. Much better that one of the largest flags in the world should continue to be flown over one of the largest squares in the world, testifying, night and day, to the greatness of Mexico. During the evening paper kites resembling birds of prey were flown over the Zócalo, at times appearing to dive-bomb the flag. At the foot of the pole a single drum was being beaten by a long-haired Indian, flanked by two girls holding incense cups aloft. The flag flew on after midnight, by which time the square had emptied and I retired to bed.

❧ Mexican Habits Die Hard ❧

It was now Sunday morning, and at about four-thirty I was woken up by an absurdly amplified voice coming from the square. It was calling out numbers – I could only presume it was the national lottery – but instead of the six numbers which make up the lottery in Britain, these went on and on, interrupted every few minutes by loud canned music. Who would want to check their numbers at this hour? (I was told later that no one actually wins the lottery, because any winner would inevitably be held to ransom by *pistoleros*.) Equally bizarrely, when I looked out of the window, the mighty flag was no longer at the top of its pole. Before six o'clock the bugles and drums were sounding again from the palace for the ceremonial dawn flag-raising, and my short night was over. Not long afterwards, the yo-yo procedure of the previous evening resumed and the flag came down again. Military cadets now began to arrive in the square in army lorries for what I later learnt was the ceremony of *jura de la bandera*, the taking of the military oath before the national flag. It was attended by hundreds of school-leavers, red-baseball-capped and wearing jeans and white T-shirts, who were about to be conscripted; also young female *voluntarias* who carried red and gold banners and shook in the chill of early morning. When, an hour or so later, the flag was raised again for the benefit of the assembled mass of Mexican youth, the presidential buglers and drummers were joined by trombones and tubas. Together they made a magnificent martial noise to fire the hearts of the next Mexican military generation. The cadets and the baseball-capped students saluted while the great flag rose gently up the pole and fluttered benevolently over them all. More national flags flew from the palace and other buildings round the square. It was a stirring sight for a Sunday morning.

One reason for the significance of the flag in the middle of the Zócalo is that the square has no great central statue. General Santa Anna was apparently intending to build a monument to independence, but he never got further than the plinth (which is the literal meaning of *zócalo*). However, the presidential palace and the cathedral make this the political and religious centre of the city, and so much of Mexican life is here. On any day, while the demonstrators against slum living or police violence shuffle by and the war-painted Aztecs stamp and dance, you will find a few people on the pavement outside the cathedral offering themselves for work and advertising their skills – *electricista, plomero de gaz, pintor de casas*.

Mass was being celebrated almost continuously throughout the day in the lopsided cathedral, permanently under repair since it was damaged both by fire in the 1960s and by earthquake in the 1980s. (It does not, of course, draw as many people as the modern basilica of Guadalupe, on the outskirts of the city, which, despite resembling a vast warehouse, is the most revered shrine in Latin America. But a visit to both buildings enables one to understand the saying that seventy-five per cent of Mexicans are Catholic and the other twenty-five per cent are very Catholic.) By nightfall, as the last mass of the day was ending, the armed auxiliary police outside the cathedral were waiting to go home, and the jobseekers who had failed to get work were leaving for what passed for home. A soap-box speaker was declaiming on the subject of the students still in gaol months after their arrest for throwing stones at the American embassy. One of those listening was dressed in Red Cross uniform. He rested a hand on the shoulder of an old lady in a shawl, who was tired out after spending the day offering a few knick-knacks for sale from a cardboard box. Daily life in the Zócalo reveals traits of the Mexican character other than a propensity for violence and corruption. There is patience, dignity and pride, religious faith, fatalism, and a wry amusement at the way of things in Mexico. There was no real expectation that the new Presidente Fox could make much difference; but, as the worshippers, the vendors, the unemployed artisans, the beggars and the police left the cathedral steps for the night, they could see that their flag was still flying.

Zócalo, Mexico City

Chapter IX
A Brighter Border Future?

A MEXICAN woman journalist was telling me of the time she attended a smart dinner party in New York, at which the other guests assumed her to be Spanish, or at any rate European. When she mentioned that she was Mexican, the table reacted, she said, as if she had confessed to having AIDS. The warmth which had been shown towards her earlier in the evening was no longer there. What she objected to was that among 'Anglo' society in the United States there is a stereotyping of Mexicans which hasn't changed since America, recognising its 'manifest destiny', wrested half their territory from them in 1848. But there are plenty of Americans who are ignorant of that historical event, as they are ignorant of and arrogant about Mexican culture. They still look upon Mexicans as a dishonest, indolent and intellectually inferior people. Less than a century ago, Mexican Americans were so sensitive about their identity that when they formed community organisations they took care to omit any reference to 'Mexican' in their titles. (LULAC, the League of United Latin-American Citizens, the Knights of America and the Order of the Sons of America are cases in point.) Today Mexican Americans are less oppressed, and there are a lot more of them. My journalist acquaintance said there was no ill-feeling among Mexicans about the loss of their land; they can point instead to the fact of the growing Hispanic populations in their former states of Upper California and Texas. She characterised her attitude to the United States as a 'hate-love' relationship, the love being directed towards all those things at which America is better than Mexico. If she saw two bottles of shampoo, one made in America and the other in Mexico, for sale in a supermarket at the same price, she readily admitted she would buy the American one.

The American sense of superiority over, and responsibility for, Mexico and the rest of Latin America goes back to 1823 and the Monroe Doctrine, which put the whole continent under United States tutelage. The Doctrine resulted from the young republic's fears that Europe might attempt to recolonise the American continent, in particular those countries which had until recently belonged to Spain. Keeping Europe out of the Americas, President Monroe said, was critical to the protection of Latin America's independence. But the policy was designed rather more to protect the United States' own interests, which were to ensure that the continent remained exclusively in its sphere of influence. Its appropriation of the name of the continent (America) as its own has always been resented by Latin Americans, to whom 'America' is the Americas and who refer to what we call an American as an *estadounidense*. President Taft thought of Latin Americans as 'naughty children who are exercising all the rights and privileges of grown-ups' – an attitude which still persists today, even though, at least in Washington, they may try not to be seen to be so patronising.

Interference by the US government in what Mexico sees as its own affairs is not welcomed. This occurs most controversially in the annual 'certification' process, by which the US president sends Congress a list of those countries which are to be certified as having cooperated, or not cooperated, in striving to bring an end to the trade in illegal drugs. Any countries judged uncooperative would be ineligible to receive US aid and trade-credit guarantees. The fact that Mexico has always been positively certified, even in the year that the head of its anti-drugs squad was arrested for corruption a few weeks before the certification was due, is beside the point. Mexico has always objected to the unilateral nature of the judgment passed by a country which does little to try and reduce the demand for such drugs among its people. In Mexico's opinion, there is no right to moral authority here, and not a little hypocrisy. True, something like two thirds of Colombia's cocaine production passes through Mexico to the United States, not to mention large quantities of heroin originating in Mexico. But there is more marijuana produced in the state of California than in Mexico, and in 2001 opium-poppy production in Mexico was reported at its lowest level for years. Demand is fed by the seemingly insatiable desire of Americans to smoke, inhale and inject an enormous variety of drugs. Is it to be Mexico's, rather than America's, responsibility to control that desire? The certification process, said one Mexican minister in the last year of the Clinton administration, was also disrespectful and offended national pride.

When Vicente Fox became president in 2000, perhaps the first ever with an authentic democratic mandate to modernise and reform his country, he had the abolition of the annual certification process high on his agenda. The drug industry was driven by the appetite of Americans, he told President George W. Bush at their first presidential meeting in February 2001, and that appetite was responsible in large part for the drug cartels and the culture of corruption in Mexico. Mr Bush apparently acknowledged this – though he could hardly be expected to take the blame for the fact that Mexico is endemically corrupt – and agreed that the two nations must work together against the drugs problem in future and not apportion blame. A bill before Congress, introduced by a Texan senator, to exempt Mexico from drug certification was never going to be passed in time to suspend the process in 2001. Nor would resistance from the majority of senators be easily overcome. But the joint initiative on drugs was put in place, headed by the US Attorney-General and Mexico's National Security Adviser, and it was suggested that unilateral certification should be suspended for three years and in future should be a matter not only for the United States but for the whole continent, decided by the Organization of American States.

What did emerge more clearly from that first meeting between presidents was a commitment to develop 'an orderly framework for migration'. In one of his first statements after winning the election in July 2000, Fox spoke of an open border between Mexico and the USA within in ten years, citing the example of migration within the European Union which should be replicated by the NAFTA countries. It may be no more than a dream, a vision for the foreseeable future, but it gave notice to the US administration that Fox was serious about the immigrant question and would not leave it alone. The day after he became president, Fox invited the Governor of Arizona and Lieutenant-Governor of Texas, together with leaders of migrant and other Mexican-American groups, to a meeting at his official residence. Two weeks later he was at the border in Ciudad Juárez, making clear to customs officials that their traditional practice of extracting *mordidas* from the queues of migrants returning to Mexico for Christmas would no longer be tolerated. The following month the senior customs officers in all the border towns, from Tijuana to Matamoros, were replaced.

Fox began doing things differently on the day of his inauguration. During the previous seven decades, all presidents had, at the very least, maintained their distance from the church – if they did not try and destroy it. But on the morning of 1 December 2000, the incoming president made a point of going to pray and take communion at the Basilica of Guadalupe just before his investiture. Later that day, wearing a zipped jerkin, he walked informally among the huge crowds in the Zócalo. (Unfortunately, old-fashioned Mexico was present elsewhere in the city centre when, a few hours earlier, demonstrators, not against Fox, were kicked and beaten in the street by riot police with truncheons.)

A Brighter Border Future?

In his first week, President Fox spoke of the eighteen million Mexicans living beyond their country's borders.

> It seems to me that when someone anywhere in the world decides to leave his home with only his mind, his heart and his passion for improvement as preparation, he has to be the most admirable person alive. If we want to see what's behind such a person, we will find, for the most part, the values that lead to success: determination, courage, bravery, passion and love.

All Mexicans, he said, should become infected with the same spirit, but in future should be able to realise their dreams in their own country. Noble sentiments indeed; but for the present, and the recent past, one can do no better than cite the admirable example of those Mexicans who have gone to the place which they like to call (using the presumed Aztec form) Manhattitlan.

It was while Luz Maria Montaño was in New York, as wife of the then Mexican ambassador to the United Nations, that she became aware of the increasing number of immigrants from her country who were coming to work in the city. There had been hardly any in 1970, but soon afterwards the migration to Manhattan began, and by the 1990s hundreds of thousands could be seen on the streets of the metropolis each year to celebrate Mexico's national day, and the image of Our Lady of Guadalupe took up residence in St Patrick's Cathedral. New York became the third most popular state for immigrants, after California and Texas. As a researcher at the Humanities Coordination of the National University of Mexico, Señora Montaño made enquiries among this new immigrant population and learnt that almost all of them came from the same part of Mexico: the states of Puebla, Guerrero and Oaxaca, east and south of Mexico City. There was a town called Tehuixtla which became known as Little New York because almost all its younger inhabitants had gone to live there. Most of the migrants crossed the border at Tijuana and, as the flow increased and a network was built up, arrangements were made to provide them with flights on to New York, temporary lodging and information about jobs. The interdependence among people from the same region was such that soon a third of new arrivals had jobs waiting for them. Restaurants, dry cleaners, fruit and vegetable shops, often owned by Koreans, became popular places of employment for Mexicans. (Other migrants, coming mostly from Michoacan and Jalisco, south-west of Mexico City, found jobs in New Jersey, especially as gardeners and in country clubs.)

Something like eight billion dollars is repatriated every year by immigrants. In the towns and villages of Puebla, thanks to income earned in New York, schools have been built, streets paved, drainage provided, churches restored. Houses have been built with brick instead of adobe, local parks have been given equipment for children's playgrounds. One town acquired three pizzerias, opened by people who had worked in the business for years in New York. Better conditions and employment opportunities at home will, it is hoped, slow the rate of migration northwards. Among the major individual success stories, one undocumented immigrant ended up supplying most of New York's tortillas, made with corn from Illinois. Another, Jaime Luzero, left his Puebla village, Independencia, when he was eight years old and his father died. He lived and did jobs in a parking lot in northern Mexico for some years before making his way to the USA and to New York, where he was to become the leading importer of designer clothes.

The Manhattan Mexicans have been assisted by a more flexible approach from the authorities to their undocumented state than they would have found elsewhere in the USA, largely due to the climate of multi-culturalism which New York's then mayor, Mario Cuomo, liked to foster. It was during Cuomo's time that a group of illegal Mexican immigrants once held a demonstration protesting at police who had stopped them selling chewing-gum in the streets. It was quite an example, one might think, of Mexican chutzpah: the police could have rounded them all up and sent them back home. But the demonstrators won, and the chewing-gum went back on sale. Señora Montaño was given a cartoon depicting a party of Aztecs sailing up the Hudson River to conquer Manhattitlan. They have certainly displayed the qualities – determination, courage, passion – characterised by President Fox as the attributes that lead to success.

The determination to get to the United States is, of course, fired by economic inequality and will continue for as long as the wage gap for manual labour remains as wide as it is (a US daily rate of approximately $60, compared with $5 in Mexico). Land degradation, due in part to persistent drought and population growth (much higher in rural areas than in the cities), is another factor in persuading people to head north. They will need all their determination and courage when they get to and across the border, suffering at the hands of coyotes or *polleros*, people-smugglers who charge up to two thousand dollars for escorting each *indocumentado* to the USA and then often abandon them, and even tip off the Border Patrol, before they have reached the relative safety of a town or major highway. Further abuse may follow if they are detained by Border Patrol agents or vigilante US farmers. Allegations of rape, beatings and general ill-treatment and harassment are widespread and have been documented by Amnesty International. In one case, a Mexican who had been arrested at San Ysidro, the border crossing between Tijuana and San Diego, was transferred to a hospital in Mission Valley where he was found to have both AIDS and TB. During his three-month stay he was kept chained and handcuffed to the bed, on orders from the Border Patrol, and denied visitors. One night, two BP agents came to the hospital to remove the patient, in spite of protests from nurses that he needed further treatment. He was taken away, wearing only a hospital gown and without being allowed to collect his clothes and money. He was then dumped over the border and, almost too weak to walk, was fortunate to find a kindly taxi driver who took him to hospital in Tijuana. As Rita Vargas, one of the Mexican consuls along the California border, put it tactfully to me, 'We have problems with some Border Patrol agents who do not interpret correctly the US–Mexican agreements for dealing with illegal immigrants.' But she acknowledged that relations with senior BP officials were good on the whole.

The United States does not have an impressive record in its treatment of Mexicans, in spite of their rights being given explicit protection a hundred and fifty years ago by the Treaty of Guadalupe Hidalgo. They are still generally treated as second-class citizens in American society, and as a good deal lower than that when they try to enter the United States illegally. Border restrictions will of course remain for the foreseeable future, but the time seems to be approaching when the Tortilla Curtain, the high steel or wire fence recalling East and West Germany, will no longer be acceptable. After all, most of the border cities enjoy good relations with each other (taking a European example, they are better than relations between Gibraltar and La Linea or Algeciras). The mayors get together, the governors of adjoining border states have regular meetings, Good Neighbour Commissions have been set up. And in 2001 significant measures were being taken to alleviate the lot of the illegal immigrant. The Border Patrol had stopped using live ammunition in the course of their duties; and some sympathetic Americans had begun to establish water stations for dehydrated Mexicans in the California and Arizona deserts. More Mexican consulates in the border towns should in future make for better communication with US authorities.

Undoubtedly, Presidents Bush and Fox are in large part responsible for this changing attitude. When Bush, who speaks Spanish and has a Mexican sister-in-law, was governor of Texas, he was instrumental in the building of new international bridges across the Rio Grande, and he worked to reduce the level of pollution in the river. He provided Mexico with access to water when it was hit by drought, and he championed a programme to help Mexico fight tuberculosis along the border. He and Fox have known one another since the mid-1990s and they are friends. Bush has a good record on cross-border issues; there is reason to expect that he and Fox will tackle together the big issues of immigration and drugs.

Vicente Fox is not like other Mexican presidents. He is serious about the border, treating immigration and drugs as problems for Mexico as well as for the USA. His dream of an open border should come as no great surprise. He grew up, as one of nine children, in Guanajuato (the state with the highest number of short-term migrants to the USA), where his family grew, and still grows, broccoli, cauliflower and Brussels sprouts for sale across the Rio Grande. Fox's party, PAN (Partido Accion Nacional), made its first breakthrough in the north in the 1980s, in effect wresting control of the border state of Chihuahua from the party (PRI) which had ruled the country for almost sixty years. (Needless to say, the PRI soon regained power by means of blatant electoral fraud.)

Fox likes to use the example of Europe to persuade the USA to anticipate the day when economic convergence will enable border restrictions to be lifted and mass migration between Mexico and America will be no more than a memory. He quotes the experience of Germany which, twenty-five years ago, was flooded with immigrants from the Iberian Peninsula but which today has no such problem with other European Union countries. (The immigrant problem comes now from the east.) To this end, Fox proposes the creation of a development fund through NAFTA and the North American Development Bank to help the jobs market and raise income levels in Mexico.

In Fox's first year, Citicorp bought Mexico's second largest bank and the prospects for new foreign investment were looking good, particularly from US retail groups, who took the decision to open stores south of the border. And when the British prime minister, Tony Blair, visited Mexico in August 2001, a substantial trade delegation accompanied him. Mexico's exports to the USA had been increasing by about twenty per cent a year since NAFTA came into effect in 1994, and Mexico had become America's second trading partner, ahead of Japan. But the slowdown in the US economy inevitably began to have its effect on its southern neighbour, with Daimler/Chrysler announcing in early 2001 that over the next three years it would close three of its car plants in Mexico. Simultaneously, Mexico began selling electricity to California, leading to speculation that the countries might work towards a common energy policy. Substantially larger foreign reserves than in 1994 helped to allay fears of another *crisis sexenal*, yet Fox did say, in the middle of 2001 and only half-jokingly, 'We need to pray to the Virgin of Guadalupe that the US economy recovers.' More seriously, he began to be criticised for having promised reforms which he was failing to deliver.

The pattern of economic development along the border was beginning to change as the *maquiladora* concept came under review and was even considered by some to be heading for redundancy. With the ending of their preferred status in 2006, many *maquilas* were heading south, to other parts of Mexico, and to countries such as Haiti and the Dominican Republic, to take advantage of cheaper labour costs. Others were converting to full production units on the border, with Mexican as well as foreign investment. A former governor of Baja California (born in San Diego), Ernesto Ruffo Appel, was appointed Border Commissioner to tackle economic and infrastructure problems in the border cities and to protect the rights of migrating Mexicans, in particular against the depredations of the *polleros*, many of whom are in league with corrupt Mexican officials. But he had no remit across the border.

A Brighter Border Future?

Bi-national responsibility for the border region – for crime and violence, environmental pollution, infrastructure, shared resources such as water – was the aim of a Mexican–US committee formed in 2001, without government sponsorship. Some members of this committee had contributed to a report on the status of illegal migrants, published in 2001 under the auspices of the Carnegie Endowment for International Peace. Membership of the panel included, from Mexico, Andres Rozental, a former ambassador to Britain and the United Nations, and, until he became foreign minister, Jorge Castañeda, Rozental's half-brother. On the US side were President Clinton's former chief of staff, Thomas ('Mack') McLarty, and the Bishop of Camden, Nicholas DiMarzio. There were academics, lawyers and union leaders from both countries.

The committee addressed the question of immigration as a shared responsibility because of changes taking place in both countries which encouraged serious negotiation, almost for the first time. It was not just that both incoming presidents intended to put immigration high on their agendas. In 2000, the largest American labour union, AFL–CIO, and the Federal Reserve chairman, Alan Greenspan, were effectively saying that the US economy needed more immigrant workers – a hugely significant change of tune. The approaching retirement of the baby-boom generation also meant that a smaller US workforce would be available in the coming years. In Mexico it was noted that the demographic profile was changing. Whereas in 2000 more than half the population was under twenty-five (the age group most likely to make the hazardous trek across the border to find work), over the next two decades the birth rate is expected to continue to decline. The proportion of middle-aged people will therefore rise and, assuming sustained growth in the Mexican economy, the migration graph should start to fall.

On both sides of the border there was increasing concern for the denial of rights to Mexican workers illegally in the USA. What this committee was most concerned to achieve was some form of legal status for the majority of the several million *indocumentados* living in the USA, an agreed guest-worker programme providing for temporary residence of a period of months, and the granting of equal rights – social-security benefits, workers' compensation schemes – to Mexicans. It also wanted Mexicans removed from the quota system which currently permits no more immigrant visas to be handed out each year to Mexico, or to America's other neighbour, Canada, than to any other country. This would surely be no more than fair to one of the two countries which, through NAFTA, already enjoy a special economic relationship with America. Visas for short-term migration, known as 'circularity', would not only be the favoured option for both Mexico and America, but would help to reverse the recent pattern of immigration. Tougher measures taken by the Border Patrol to restrict immigrant numbers have discouraged them from risking the journey every year, and families have been losing their sons for good. No one pretends that illegal crossings will be ended, but it is hoped that the two countries will cooperate to combat the criminal networks of people-smugglers, to save lives and to help develop viable border communities.

President Fox in effect adopted these proposals when he received the committee's report at the time of his first presidential meeting with Bush, who came to Mexico in February 2001. And he was hoping for some agreement to be announced on immigration when he made a state visit to Washington later that year. The atmosphere was cosy – Fox called Bush 'Jorge' and Bush welcomed him to the 'Casa Blanca' for a dinner of crab and chorizo, bison with a pumpkin seed crust, and a tequila and chile sabayon – when they met again at the beginning of September, but it was clear before Fox left Mexico City that no deal was imminent. The question of potential green-card status for Mexican guest workers and immigrants illegally resident in the USA was proving 'complex' – not least because Bush would have a hard time getting such proposals through Congress. Nevertheless, the two presidents appeared to have reached an understanding that the immigrant's lot would soon be a happier one. Bush told Fox that 'the United States has no more important relationship in the world than our relationship with Mexico'.

Less than a week later, more than three thousand people were killed by suicide bombers flying airliners into the twin towers of the World Trade Center in New York and the Pentagon in Washington, and things were different. Security was, of course, increased on America's southern border (it was thought that some of the hijackers had crossed the Canadian border overland from Quebec to Maine), and the consequent delays had an immediate effect on business in the border towns. Commerce generally fell by around fifty per cent, even affecting the Boys' Town prostitutes whose earnings were sharply reduced when Americans found it took many hours to cross and recross the border for a few minutes of doubtful pleasure. However, it did not take long for tourism in the US border towns to improve as the American south-west was viewed as a relatively safe place to go. The economic downturn and resulting recession in the USA hit jobs in Mexico – in the *maquiladoras*, in the car industry, in tourism – as well as employment prospects for Mexicans north of the border. Fox had been speaking of an annual growth target of seven per cent, but after September 11th the forecast for growth in 2001 was zero. Increased unemployment in the Mexican border towns caused an escalation in street crime, while greater security at the border gave the coyotes an excuse to charge even more for an escorted crossing.

Fox declared his support for the United States, and he went to Washington in early October to reiterate his country's willingness to assist in matters of intelligence and border security. But there was no question of providing military aid – in the Second World War Mexico had supplied no more than a token military presence, serving in the Philippines. 'We are not a military country,' Fox said, apparently without any ironical reference to Mexico's past. He was also mindful of the fact that sixty-two per cent of Mexicans, according to a poll, thought that Mexico should remain neutral. The old resentments and psychological hang-ups between Mexico and the USA were surfacing again. Overt cooperation with its northern neighbour indicated submission to it. Mexico had no interest in conflicts beyond its borders. The USA stole our territory and is still a bully, if not an enemy. It should not be interfering in the affairs of other countries, whether Mexico or Afghanistan. Such were the sentiments being expressed in student, working-class and some political circles in the days following September 11th. Meanwhile, Mexican Americans in Dallas were queuing up to enlist.

While Mexico's border guards were being mobilised against the threat of terrorists entering the USA from Latin America or using the border as an escape route south, drug-smugglers were finding that the heightened security made their life more difficult. So they took to off-loading drugs in the border towns, with the consequent suffering soon visible on the streets of Tijuana and Ciudad Juárez. Fox's government had already had some success in stemming corruption and the flow of weapons between the two countries. In February 2001, sixty-seven out of the eighty federal police agents in the state of Chihuahua were sacked, while with active US assistance efforts were concentrated on breaking the Arellano Felix cartel in Tijuana (where the proposal to change the city's telephone area code to 666, with its bestial associations in the Bible [Revelation 13:18], was viewed as a joke in particularly bad taste). Plastic surgeons were urged by the Mexican drug-enforcement agency to report any suspicious requests for change of identity. In Sinaloa, 'narco-ballads', by groups such as Los Tigres del Norte, singing of drug-traffickers bribing politicians, were banned from the airwaves. The FBI were delighted when, early in 2002, the Mexican authorities shot dead one of the Arellano Felix brothers and arrested another; but within days the name of Ismael Zambada was being mentioned as the man most likely in fill the power vacuum. No one expected there to be anything but a temporary interruption in the flow of drugs through Tijuana into the USA.

On immigration, the foreign minister, Jorge Castañeda, said shortly before September 11th that 'we are going for the whole *enchilada*' – legalisation of the status of undocumented immigrants, provision of guest-worker visas for up to a year to Mexicans taking jobs in American agricultural and service industries and the possibility for immigrants of achieving green-card status. But in the immediate aftermath of September 11th it was doubtful whether they would get more than a tortilla chip – though Bush did insist that the understanding previously reached with Fox was still on his agenda. Norman Mailer had a phrase about Mexico: 'The mournfulness of unrequited injustice hangs a shroud across the centuries,' which could be applied equally to the plight of Mexican immigrants to the USA. Anyone who is fit and has enough determination can cross the border and get a job, but once there – in places like California's Central Valley, where so many of the *indocumentados* live – poverty is widespread and any workers' rights are denied them. Every year at least three hundred thousand are likely to be poisoned by pesticides and other agricultural chemicals.

None of this will change until the *enchilada* negotiated between Presidents Bush and Fox is brought back to the table. (Tentative talks between Castañeda and the US Secretary of State, Colin Powell, were resumed in January 2002. Powell reiterated that he was still committed to immigration reforms, but at the end of 2002, following a high-level binational meeting in Mexico City, no early progress on the issue was anticipated; and Castañeda became so frustrated that he handed in his resignation.) Wide-ranging improvements are also required within Mexico: in education – raising the school-leaving age above twelve – and in living standards. Assuming the continued success of NAFTA

A Brighter Border Future?

and an economic growth rate which will recover from US recession and the shock of the terrorist attacks, it is possible to envisage a narrowing of the wages gap between the two countries, as has happened within western Europe, to the extent that migration pressures are no longer significant. Then – who knows? – in twenty-five to thirty years the Mexican–US border may be as open as the border with Canada, which would only be consistent with free trade and globalisation. Post-September 11th there was talk in the USA of bringing some consistency of approach, in the longer term, to both its northern and southern borders, with a 'security perimeter' to cover airports, ports and Mexico's southern border with Guatemala and Belize.

Fox, of course, cannot be president beyond 2006. Yet the *honestidad valiente* which he has begun to bring to Mexican political life is likely to be sustained. It is significant, for instance, that since 2000 none of the media has been in receipt of government subsidy. The former mouthpieces of the old ruling party (PRI) are now independent, often hostile to the government and, in some cases, which is the price of freedom, in financial trouble. Taking again the example of Europe, there are those who, anticipating the trend towards economic and political convergence, look forward to the day when Tijuana and San Diego have a common airport, operating for both countries as Geneva does for Switzerland and France. It is not an impossible dream.

Envoi

FOR A previous book, *Spanish Hours*, I travelled through old, interior Spain, away from the cosmopolitan cities and the overdeveloped coastal resorts, and wrote about the enduring characteristics of the country and its people. Until the Spanish left in the early years of the nineteenth century, Mexico was known as New Spain, and in my journey along the border, I have often been reminded of those legacies, which are of course old Spanish today. There are the place-names, the churches and the influence of the Catholic Church and, one of the aspects of life in Mexico (and elsewhere in Latin America) which go to the heart of Spanish culture, the bulls.

Of all the reasons for cross-border intercourse between Mexico and the USA – both within and outside the law – bullfighting is the one with the most directly Spanish origins. Of course, bullfighting is good for tourism, but at a more serious level it fosters relationships across the border not only between Mexicans and Mexican Americans but between Mexicans and Anglos. In October 2001, two events were held, one in Tlaxcala, near Mexico City, the other in Reynosa, on the Rio Grande. Tlaxcala hosted a convention of the National Association of Taurine Clubs of the United States, with club representation from Los Angeles, Chula Vista, San Francisco and El Paso. In Reynosa, the International Association of Aficionados Practicos (those who enjoy trying their hand at caping young animals) held a three-day festival, with entertainments on both sides of the border. One Texan enthusiast,

❖ Envoi ❖

Fred Renk, has established a bullring on his ranch in Starr County, where he runs a bullfighting school and holds bloodless fights. Whatever one may think of the spectacle of the bulls, I like to believe it has a not-insignificant role to play in improving cross-border relationships and thus helping to bring down the Tortilla Curtain.

I observed earlier that, at the municipal level, relationships across the border, and especially across the Rio Grande, are better than they are in Europe between Gibraltar and Spain. To Spain, Gibraltar constitutes a wart on the bottom of its peninsula, and I wonder whether the mistrust between the two, based on disputed sovereignty, will ever disappear – whether or not sovereignty of the Rock is to be shared in future between Britain and Spain. There has been no dispute over sovereignty between Mexico and the USA for a hundred and fifty years, but there are those Americans who think of Mexico as if not a wart at least a rash of septic spots infecting its southern border. Many Border Patrol agents certainly think so. And there is no denying that Mexicans export their standard of living to the USA, making the south Texan towns of the Rio Grande River valley among the poorest in the Union.

The people and the shacks and the country on one side of the Los Ebanos ferry may be indistinguishable from the people and the shacks and the country across the Rio Grande on the other side; and the Mexican–Texan settlements of Donna may not look much different from the poor *colonias* of Reynosa. But you have only to go downtown, or to the main highways, on either side of the river for the First World/Third World divide to be at once evident. Of course, for the long-distance traveller well-made American roads with several lanes and frequent service areas are preferable to much of the Mexican road network, and it is easier to find your way in the grid pattern of American city streets than in the maze and straggle of streets in a Mexican town, with few signposts to anywhere. But then, I found myself occasionally wondering, is there not something more appealing

✧ ENVOI ✧

about the disorganisation of Mexican roads, something endearing about their lack of order and First-World facilities?

It is not a wholly perverse question. For while the countless advantages of the First World over the Third are obvious enough, it is the unique juxtaposition here of the developed and developing worlds that can bring into focus some the latter's virtues. On the Mexican side of the line, as the policeman was anticipating in Graham Greene's story, 'Across the Bridge', there is 'life'. Much of it may be seedy, or squalid, and may lead to premature death; but it is more exciting, and certainly more unpredictable, than the life to be found in a cheerless US motel selling root beer and weak coffee or in the adobe-style *casitas* of those gated communities for retired Americans near the Arizona border south of Tucson. This is the life which the First World can provide, settled and safe and uneventful, with few risks other than from a defective hairdryer or a mis-hit golf ball. In the United States, the First World seems to provide an anaesthetised, polythene-wrapped existence which no warm-blooded Latino, from whichever world, would wish to share.

The misery of life for many in the Third World may be unrelieved, lacking the hygiene, water, electricity, medicine which many of us have taken for granted all our lives. But the Mexican way of life, at all economic levels, does have compensations which more 'mature' societies may envy. There is, for instance, the strong family structure, much of it inherited from the Mexican's Spanish and Indian origins, which binds not only the nuclear family but also the parents' siblings – and particularly the mother's sisters. There may as yet be little respect for women's rights in Mexican society, but within the family they are accorded the greatest respect for their traditional roles. To say of someone that 'no tiene madre' (he has no mother) means that he is not an honourable man. Mother's Day has a much greater significance in Mexico than in most First-World countries; on this day most families take their mothers out, bringing traffic to a halt and filling every restaurant in town.

⇝ Envoi ⇜

The use of one's mother's surname, as in Spain, after one's father's, illustrates the same point. (Outside the family, however, machismo still often prevails and women may suffer. Male behaviour at the expense of women in its most extreme form resulted in serial killings in Ciudad Juárez, unsolved and still going on in 2002, a phenomenon referred to as 'feminocide'.)

Mexican marriage customs, in some sections of society, have much to recommend them over First-World practices. When a man wishes to marry, the request is often made by his father to the girl's father. Or in some regions it may be made on the young man's behalf by a *portador*, a man respected in the community. Traditionally, if the *portador* is told to return for an answer within a week, he may expect the girl's parents to reject the marriage proposal; more than two weeks' wait indicates approval. Within a community, too, there may be a *palomilla*, an informal network of friends, and formal bonds of friendship may be expressed between *compadres* who, like mothers, also have their annual day. Outside these associations, though, and outside the household, Mexicans tend not to be neighbourly, indeed to be distrustful of their neighbours, which may not be a bad thing. When they fall sick, they are likely to visit a *curandero*, a faith healer, whose powers are sometimes acknowledged by conventional physicians.

Admirable as these Third-World attitudes and codes of behaviour may be (they are to be found also in Chicano neighbourhoods close to the border in south Texas), they will not, of course, keep a young Mexican in Mexico, unless and until it is economically worth his while to stay. To this end, President Bush announced in March 2002 that thirty million dollars would be available for investment in those regions of rural Mexico which have the largest numbers of migrants to the USA. One may wonder whether the gap between First and Third world will ever be bridged; certainly it will not be permanently narrowed without large-scale and continuing investment in the developing country, which

❖ ENVOI ❖

includes monies repatriated from those Mexicans working in the USA. There will continue to be pressure for guest-worker permits, but this will be no more than a short-term panacea. It will encourage further illegal migration to the USA and will provide no long-term solution to the immigrant problem between adjoining First- and Third-World countries. Bush's genuine concern, however, and his relationship with President Fox, do bode well for the future, not least for a more constructive interest on the part of Americans in what goes on south of the border. Until now the American attitude in the border states – most of all in Arizona and, to a lesser extent, California – has generally been contemptuous towards Mexicans. Mexico is seen as 'uncivilised' and, like nature, red in tooth and claw, and Americans would rather not know about it, preferring to stick with the post-modernist, politically correct world which they think they understand.

And yet I have often witnessed genuine fellow feeling between the two sides, by which I mean the two sides of a line which permits and promotes interrelationships through the *mestizaje* of two peoples. I have seen it in the *amistad* ceremonies on the international bridges, in the procession for the annual Brownsville/Matamoros carnival celebrations and in informal contacts between friends. But the line also separates two ways of life, and where the line becomes a corrugated steel fence, the two sides – Mexican citizens v. US authorities – are inevitably engaged in a contest where there will be winners and losers.

When I was on the beach outside Tijuana, looking at the border fence and the columns of names of those who had died trying to make it to California, I heard a young Mexican boasting to a couple of bystanders that he could burrow under the fence, just beneath the list of his dead compatriots. Then he came over to me and, for some unexplained reason, shook my hand. Like George Orwell, who recounts at the beginning of *Homage to Catalonia*, how his hand was shaken by a stranger, an Italian militiaman, when he arrived at the barracks in

❧ Envoi ❦

Barcelona to enlist in Spain's Civil War, I was touched by the gesture – though unsure how to interpret it. The Mexican was dressed in the regulation clothes of a would-be immigrant – short-sleeved shirt, canvas shoes and a peaked baseball cap. He had a strong, open face with a look of insouciance about it. We did not speak and, as Orwell wrote, I knew 'that to retain my first impression of him I must not see him again; and needless to say I never did see him again'. But I like to think that he made it.

SELECT BIBLIOGRAPHY

Alba, Victor, *A Concise History of Mexico*, Cassell (1973)
Annerino, John, *Dead in Their Tracks*, Four Walls Eight Windows (1999)
Boyle, T. Coraghessan, *The Tortilla Curtain*, Bloomsbury (1995)
Cunninghame Graham, R.B., *The North American Sketches*, edited by John Walker, University of Alabama Press (1986)
Fuentes, Carlos, *The Crystal Frontier*, Bloomsbury (1998)
Greene, Graham, *The Lawless Roads*, Heinemann (1939)
Greene, Graham, *The Power and the Glory*, Heinemann (1940)
Horgan, Paul, *Great River: The Rio Grande in North American History*, Rinehart (1954)
Kearney, Milo and Knopp, Anthony, *Boom and Bust*, Eakin Press (1991)
Lord, Walter, *A Time to Stand*, Transworld (1964)
McCarthy, Cormac, *The Border Trilogy*, Picador (1995-98)
McLynn, Frank, *Villa and Zapata*, Jonathan Cape (2000)
Marnham, Patrick, *So Far from God*, Jonathan Cape (1985)
Martinez, Oscar J., *Troublesome Border*, University of Arizona Press (1988)
Miller, Tom, *On the Border*, University of Arizona Press (1981)
Rubel, Arthur, *Across the Tracks*, University of Texas Press (1966)
Strieber, Whitley and Kunetka, James, *Warday*, Holt, Rinehart (1984)
Tuchman, Barbara, *The Zimmermann Telegram*, Constable (1959)
Turner, John Kenneth, *Barbarous Mexico*, Cassell (1911)
Tweedie, Mrs Alec, *Mexico As I Saw It*, Hurst & Blackett (1901)
Tweedie, Mrs Alec, *From Díaz to the Kaiser*, Hutchinson (1917)
Weisman, Alan, *La Frontera*, University of Arizona Press (1986)
Wheatcroft, Andrew, *The Habsburgs*, Viking (1995)
Young, Gavin, *From Sea to Shining Sea*, Hutchinson (1995)

Index

Abrego, Juan Garcia 178, 180, 185
AFL-CIO 54, 172, 207
Agua Prieta 130-36
Ajo 145-47
Alamo, The 17
Alamo 6, 11, 12, 16, 18, 20
All the Pretty Horses 92
Alpine 95
American Civil War 43, 83
Amistad, Lake 89-90
Anapra 103
Angeles, Felipe 115
Annerino, John 149-50
Antelope Wells 129
Appel, Ernesto Ruffo 162, 206
Appomattox 36
Arruza, Carlos 165
Austin, Stephen 16
Avalon, Robert 25
Azcarraga, Emilio 183

Bagdad 38-41, 45
Balfour, Arthur 120
Balli, Nicolas 41
Barbarous Mexico 26
Bartlett, John Russell 70, 130
Bean, Judge Roy 91
Benton, William 112-13
Bermudez, Antonio J. 103
Big Bend National Park 96
Bisbee 132
Blair, Tony 206
Bonaparte, Joseph 14
Boquillas Canyon 95-96
Border Industrialization Program 61, 103

Border Patrol 36, 46, 48, 51-52, 54-55, 58, 75, 79-81, 91, 96, 98, 109, 126, 132-34, 149-50, 152-54, 169-70, 172, 177, 186, 203-204, 208
Bowie, James 11, 16-17
Boyle, T. Coraghessan 173
Brompton Cemetery 87
Brownsville 6, 35-36, 39, 41-48, 50-52, 54, 56, 71-72, 84, 117
Buchanan, President James 44
bullfights 164-65, 213-14
Bush, President George W. 7, 71, 175, 199, 204, 208, 211, 217

Cabrillo, Juan 167
Calexico 160, 162
Calles, President Plutarco Elias 30-33, 122, 130-31
Camacho, President Manuel Avila 34
Camargo 14, 66
Camino del Diablo 152, 158
Camino Real 100
Camino Real Hotel (El Paso) 109-110, 122, 131
Candelaria 99
Cárdenas, Cuauhtemoc 33, 192
Cárdenas, President Lazaro 32-33, 160
Carlota, Empress 24-25
Carnegie Endowment for International Peace 207
Carranza, President Venustiano 113-15, 117, 119-121, 130

Casillas, Alfredo 153-54
Castañeda, Jorge 207, 211
Catholic Church 22, 31, 33, 42, 46, 60
Chamizal Settlement 107
Charles III, King 14
Chihuahua 29, 30, 95, 99, 106, 111-12, 121-23, 125, 129
Chiricahua Mountains 130
Chislehurst 25
Cisneros, José 102
Cities of the Plain 93
Citicorp 205
Ciudad Acuña 89
Ciudad Juárez 61, 93, 101-107, 109, 111, 114, 121, 124, 180, 200, 210, 216
Ciudad Miguel Aleman 68
Chinese immigration 158
Clarksville 38-39
Clinton, President Bill 75, 182, 185-86, 199
Cochise 130
Cochrane, Admiral Lord 157
cockfights 162-64
Cody, Colonel William 87
Colorado 22, 35
Colorado River 19, 152, 155, 160-61
Colosio, Luis Donaldo 180-81, 184, 187
Columbus (New Mexico) 99, 126-27, 130
Confederacy 20, 43-44
Conrad, Joseph 86
Corral, Luz 122, 124
Cortina, Juan 43-45, 47
Cos, General Perfecto de 16

220

❖ Index ❖

crisis sexenal 184, 206
Cristero rebellion 32
Crockett, David 11-12, 18, 20
Crook, George 129
Cross, Meliton 42
Crossing, The 93, 127
Cuba 20, 33, 45
Cuomo, Mario 202

Del Rio 89, 92
Deming 126
Díaz, President Porfirio 22, 26-28, 86, 111, 118, 131
Donna 60-61, 214
Douglas (Arizona) 130-33, 135-36
Drugs 55, 68-69, 104-106, 109, 137, 140, 148, 177-78, 180, 182, 185-87, 198-99, 205, 210
Durango 111

Eagle Mountain 99
Eagle Pass 82-84
Earp, Wyatt 167
Echeverria, President Luis 137
El Berrendo 129
El Paso 90-92, 95, 98, 100 102, 106-107, 109-110, 112, 114, 122, 125, 129-31, 173, 177
El Sahuaro 149-50, 152
Epstein, Ruth 140-41
Eugénie, Empress 23, 25

Falfurrias 59
Fannin, James 19
Felix, brothers Arellano 187-88, 210
Fitzsimmons, Bob 92
Ford, President Gerald 137
Ford, Major 'Rip' 44-45
Fort Bliss 98, 115, 177

Fort Brown 42-44, 49
Fort Casamata 115
Fort Stockton 98
Fox, President Vicente 7, 34, 77, 148, 162, 175, 188-89, 195, 199-201, 204-205, 208-209, 211-12, 217
Franklin Mountains 101
Fremont, Captain 158
Fuentes, Amado Carrillo 185, 187
Fuentes, Carlos 12, 154, 182

Gadsden Hotel (Douglas) 131
Gadsden Purchase 22, 125, 132
Garza, Filemon 42
Gates, Bill 182
Germany 116, 118, 120-21, 160, 205
Geronimo 129-30
Gila River 131, 145
Giant 94-95
Goliad 19
González, Yolanda 45-46
González, Carlos Hank 183
Graham, Robert Cunninghame 83-87
Grant, General Ulysses S. 21, 43
Greene, Graham 12, 32, 57, 78, 163, 190, 215
Greenspan, Alan 54, 172, 207
Grey, Sir Edward 112
Guadalupe Hidalgo, Treaty of 21, 204
Guzman, Joaquin 188-89

Habsburg, Felix von 26
Hanigan, George 133-36
Hardin, John Wesley 110

Hays, Jim 52-53, 55
Hearst, William Randolph 129
Hernandez, Ezequiel 98
Hernandez, José 151
Hernandez, Roberto 183
Hidalgo 57-59
Hidalgo, Miguel 14, 192
Hill, Robert 96
Hitler, Adolf 34
Hobbs Act 136
Homage to Catalonia 217
Horn, Barry 51, 53
Houston, Sam 16-17, 19, 20
Huerta, President Victoriano 29, 111-15
Humboldt, Baron von 15

Isaacson, Jacob 138
ISDA (International Sonoran Desert Alliance) 145
Italy 15
Itúrbide, Agustín de 15

Jackson, President Andrew 157
Janos 129
Japan 114, 117-19, 206
Jiménez, Leticia 169-72
John XXIII, Pope 41
Johnson, President Lyndon 107
Joseph, Emperor Franz 23
Juarez, President Benito 23-26, 31, 39, 43, 67-88, 101, 174

Kenedy, Mifflin 38, 43
Kennedy, President John 107
Kickapoo 81
King, Richard 38, 43

❖ Index ❖

Kino, Padre Eusebio 144-45, 147
Kissinger, Henry 181
Kitching, Harold 141
Ku Klux Klan 133, 135

Labastida, Francisco 187, 188
Langtry 91, 93
Langtry, Lillie 92
Laredo 14, 45, 68, 70-72, 75, 79, 80
Lavery, Sir John 86
Lawless Roads, The 32, 78, 163
Lawrence, D. H. 143, 191-92
Ledesma, Javier 64
Lee, General Robert E. 21, 36, 43
Leopold I, King 23
Life and Times of Judge Roy Bean, The 131
Lincoln, President Abraham 7, 101
Llosa, Mario Vargas 183
Long Wolf 87
Lord, Walter 16
Los Angeles 74, 142, 158
Los Ebanos 66, 214
Lukeville 148
Luzero, Jaime 202

McAllen 41, 58-59, 173
McAllen, James 58
McCaffrey, Barry 109
McCarthy, Cormac 92, 127
Madero, President Francisco 28, 111-12, 124
Madero, Raul 124
Maher, Peter 92
Mailer, Norman 165, 211
maquiladoras 40, 61-62, 64, 71, 76, 103, 105, 126, 140, 162, 169, 175, 206, 209

Manet, Edouard 25
Manhattan 201-203
Marathon 95, 97
Marfa 95, 98
Martínez, Professor Oscar 174
Massieu, Mario Ruíz 180
Massieu Pepe Ruíz 180, 184
Matamoros 6, 21, 35, 38-47, 50-51, 55-56, 71, 115, 180
Mateos, President Adolfo López 159
Maverick, Sam 17
Maximilian, Emperor 23-26, 39, 43, 190
Mexicali 159-63, 165
Mexico City 13, 16, 19, 21, 24, 29, 34, 72, 83, 85, 98, 100, 113-14, 124, 157, 165, 175, 189-95
Milam, Benjamin 16
Miller, Tom 128
Monroe Doctrine 24, 112, 198
Monterrey 21, 76
Montaño, Luz Maria 201, 203
Morelos, José Maria 14-15
Mormons 158

Naco 136-38
NAFTA (North American Free Trade Agreement) 34, 59, 61, 71, 79, 140, 142, 182, 186, 200, 205-206, 211
Napoleon III 23-25
Neale, William 41
Neil, Colonel 16-17
New York 200-203
Nicolas II, Czar 118
Nixon, President Richard 89
Nogales (Arizona and Sonora) 117, 136-38, 140-42, 144, 184
Nuevo Laredo 72-73, 75-80

Núñez, Alvar, Cabeza de Vaca 13, 98

O'Brian, Patrick 157
Obregón, President Alvaro 30-31, 113-14, 121-22, 131
Ojinaga 98-99
Oklahoma! 138
Olympic Games (1968) 34
Oñate, Juan de 100
On the Border 128
Ordaz, President Gustavo Díaz 89, 107
Orozco, Pascual 111, 114
Orwell, George 217-18

Palmito Ranch, Battle of 36, 44
Palomas 126-27
Panama Canal 118
PAN (Partido de Accion Nacional) 24, 205
Papago (Tohono O'odham) 142-43, 146
parrot smuggling 137
Patton, George 126
Pershing, General 99, 121-22, 128
Piedras Negras 81-4
Pinal, Sylvia 49
Polk, President James 20, 22
Posadas, Cardinal 180
Powell, Colin 211
Power and the Glory, The 32
Presidio 98-99
PRI (Partido Revolucionario Institucional) 34, 180, 183-84, 187, 205, 212
Pro, Father 32
Puerto Penasco (Rocky Point) 148

Querétaro 24

❖ Index ❖

Rebeldes, Los 105
Rebollo, General Jesus Gutierrez 106, 185, 187
Redford 97-98
Reichstadt, Duke of 23
Reinosa 14
Renk, Fred 214
Reynosa 57, 61, 65, 188, 213
Rio Conchos 98
Rio Grande 6, 13, 16, 21, 24, 35, 38, 42, 45, 47, 50, 55, 57, 64, 66, 67, 72, 80-81, 95-98, 100, 107, 111, 125, 160, 173
Rio Grande City 66, 69
Rivera, Diego 191
Roma 69
Rockefeller, Eileen 122
Roosevelt, President Franklin D. 34, 96, 160
Roosevelt, President Theodore 12, 115, 119
Rozental, Andres 207

Sabinas River 15
Salinas, President Carlos 33, 180-84
Salinas, Raul 180, 184-85
San Antonio 11-13, 16, 21, 51
San Antonio del Bravo 99
San Antonio River 19
San Diego 6, 157, 166-68, 170, 212
San Jacinto River 19
San Juan del Valle 60
San Luis 152-53
Santa Anna, President Antonio Lopez de 16, 19-22, 194
Santa Ysabel 115-16
Sasabe 136
Serra, Junipero 167
Shafter 95

Shaw, George Bernard 86, 175
Shelby, Joseph O. 83
Sierra del Carmen 96
Sierra del Pinacate 149
Sierra Madre 129
Sierra Vieja 99
Slim, Carlos 181, 183
Sonoyta 145, 148, 151
Spectator, The 112-13
Steidinger, Jimmy 59
Stillman, Charles 41
Study Butte 97

Taft, President William 118, 122, 131, 198
Tampico 39, 115
Taylor, General Zachary 21, 36, 42, 46
Tecate 165-66, 170
Tehuixtla 201
Tiffany, Louis 109, 131
Tijuana 6, 165-66, 168-70, 180, 184, 188, 202-204, 210, 212
Time to Stand, A 16
Tlaxcala 213
Torreon 30, 62, 113, 117
Tortilla Curtain, The 173
Traffic 184
Travis, William 11, 17
Trotsky, Leon 33
Turner, John Kenneth 26
Tweedie, Commander 113
Tweedie, Mrs Alec 27-28, 85-86

Valdes, President Miguel Aleman 34
Valentino, Rudolf 159
Vargas, Rita 204
Veracruz 19-21, 23, 28, 53, 65, 113

Victoria, Queen 24-25, 157
Villa, Pancho 28-29, 43, 47, 98-99, 110-17, 120-24, 126, 128, 130, 146
Viva Zapata 29, 69

Washington, President George 73
Weygand, General Maxime 25
Why 147-48
Wilhelm II, Kaiser 117-19
Wilson, President Woodrow 30, 43, 112-16, 119, 130
World Trade Center 209

Yaqui 26
Yashiro, Admiral 118
Young, Gavin 6
Yucatán 62
Yuma 152-53, 155

Zacatecas 30, 133
Zaffirini, Judith 74
Zambada, Ismael 211
Zapata, Emiliano 29-30, 113-14
Zedillo, President Ernesto 71, 180, 183-84, 186-87
Zimmermann, Arthur 119-20
Zuniga, Fray Garcia de San Francisco y 101-102

First published in Great Britain by

LIBRI MUNDI/ELLIOTT & THOMPSON
27 John Street
London WC1N 2BX

© Simon Courtauld 2003

The right of Simon Courtauld to be identified as the author of this work has been asserted by him in accordance with the Copyright Designs and Patents Act 1988.

Permission to quote from *The Lawless Roads* by Graham Greene granted by Random House

No part of this publication may be reproduced, stored in a retrieval system or transmitted, in any form or by any means, electronic, mechanical, photocopying, recording or otherwise, without the prior permission of the publisher.

ISBN 1 904027 08 3

First Edition

Book design by Brad Thompson
Printed and bound in Malta by Interprint